Transient Calibration of a Groundwater-Flow Model of Chimacum Creek Basin and Vicinity, Jefferson County, Washington—A Supplement to Scientific Investigations Report 2013-5160

By Joseph L. Jones and Kenneth H. Johnson

Prepared in cooperation with Jefferson County and the Washington State Department of Ecology

Open-File Report 2013–1258

U.S. Department of the Interior
U.S. Geological Survey

U.S. Department of the Interior
SALLY JEWELL, Secretary

U.S. Geological Survey
Suzette M. Kimball, Acting Director

U.S. Geological Survey, Reston, Virginia: 2013

For more information on the USGS—the Federal source for science about the Earth,
its natural and living resources, natural hazards, and the environment—visit
http://www.usgs.gov or call 1–888–ASK–USGS

For an overview of USGS information products, including maps, imagery, and publications,
visit *http://www.usgs.gov/pubprod*

To order this and other USGS information products, visit *http://store.usgs.gov*

Suggested citation:
Jones, J.L., and Johnson, K.H., 2013, Transient calibration of a groundwater-flow model of Chimacum
Creek Basin and vicinity, Jefferson County, Washington—A supplement to Scientific Investigations
Report 2013-5160: U.S. Geological Survey Open-File Report 2013-1258, 44 p.,
http://pubs.usgs.gov/of/2013/1258.

Contents

Figures

Tables

Conversion Factors and Datums

Conversion Factors

Multiply	By	To obtain
Length		
inch (in.)	2.54	centimeter (cm)
foot (ft)	0.3048	meter (m)
mile (mi)	1.609	kilometer (km)
Area		
acre	0.4047	hectare (ha)
square mile (mi^2)	259.0	hectare (ha)
Flow rate		
acre-foot per year (acre-ft/yr)	1,233	cubic meter per year (m^3/yr)
foot per day (ft/d)	0.3048	meter per day (m/d)
cubic foot per second (ft^3/s)	0.02832	cubic meter per second (m^3/s)
inch per year (in/yr)	25.4	millimeter per year (mm/yr)
Transmissivity*		
foot squared per day (ft^2/d)	0.09290	meter squared per day (m^2/d)

*Transmissivity: The standard unit for transmissivity is cubic foot per day per square foot times foot of aquifer thickness [(ft^3/d)/ft^2]ft. In this report, the mathematically reduced form, foot squared per day (ft^2/d), is used for convenience.

Temperature in degrees Fahrenheit (°F) may be converted to degrees Celsius (°C) as follows:
°C=(°F-32)/1.8.

Datums

Vertical coordinate information is referenced to the North American Vertical Datum of 1988 (NAVD 88). Horizontal coordinate information is referenced to the North American Datum of 1983 (NAD 83).

Altitude, as used in this report, refers to distance above the vertical datum.

Well-Numbering System

Wells in Washington State are assigned a local well number that identifies each well based on its location within a township (T), range (R), section, and 40-acre tract. For example, well 29N/01W-35J01 refers to township (T. 29 N) and the range (R. 01 W) north of the Willamette Base Line and west of the Willamette Meridian. The first number following the hyphen indicates the section (35) within the township, and the letter (J) following the section number indicates the 40-acre subdivision of the section. The final two-digit number (01) uniquely distinguishes individual wells in the same 40-acre tract.

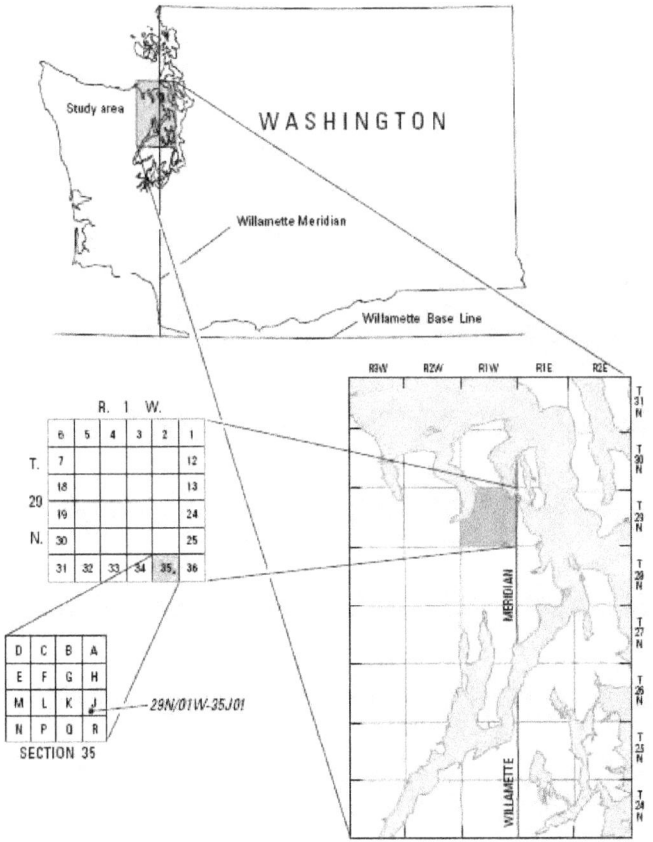

Transient Calibration of a Groundwater-Flow Model of Chimacum Creek Basin and Vicinity, Jefferson County, Washington—A Supplement to Scientific Investigations Report 2013-5160

By Joseph L. Jones and Kenneth H. Johnson

Abstract

A steady-state groundwater-flow model described in Scientific Investigations Report 2013-5160, "Numerical Simulation of the Groundwater-Flow System in Chimacum Creek Basin and Vicinity, Jefferson County, Washington" was developed to evaluate potential future impacts of growth and of water-management strategies on water resources in the Chimacum Creek Basin. This supplement to that report describes the unsuccessful attempt to perform a calibration to transient conditions on the model. The modeled area is about 64 square miles on the Olympic Peninsula in northeastern Jefferson County, Washington. The geologic setting for the model area is that of unconsolidated deposits of glacial and interglacial origin typical of the Puget Sound Lowlands. The hydrogeologic units representing aquifers are Upper Aquifer (UA, roughly corresponding to recessional outwash) and Lower Aquifer (LA, roughly corresponding to advance outwash). Recharge from precipitation is the dominant source of water to the aquifer system; discharge is primarily to marine waters below sea level and to Chimacum Creek and its tributaries.

The model is comprised of a grid of 245 columns and 313 rows; cells are a uniform 200 feet per side. There are six model layers, each representing one hydrogeologic unit: (1) Upper Confining unit (UC); (2) Upper Aquifer unit (UA); (3) Middle Confining unit (MC); (4) Lower Aquifer unit (LA); (5) Lower Confining unit (LC); and (6) Bedrock unit (OE). The transient simulation period (October 1994–September 2009) was divided into 180 monthly stress periods to represent temporal variations in recharge, discharge, and storage.

An attempt to calibrate the model to transient conditions was unsuccessful due to instabilities stemming from oscillations in groundwater discharge to and recharge from streamflow in Chimacum Creek. The model as calibrated to transient conditions has mean residuals and standard errors of 0.06 ft ±0.45 feet for groundwater levels and 0.48 ± 0.06 cubic feet per second for flows. Although the expected seasonal trends were observed in model results, the typical observed annual variation of groundwater levels of about 2 feet was not. Streamflow at the most downstream observation point was about three times larger than simulated streamflow. Because the transient version of the model proved inherently unstable, it was not used to simulate forecast conditions for alternate hydrologic or anthropogenic changes. Adaptation of alternate stream simulation packages, such as RIV, or newer versions of MODFLOW, such as MODFLOW-NWT, could possibly assist with achieving calibration to transient conditions.

Introduction

A groundwater-flow model, described in Scientific Investigations Report 2013-5160, "Numerical Simulation of the Groundwater-Flow System in Chimacum Creek Basin and Vicinity, Jefferson County, Washington," was developed in cooperation with Jefferson County and the Washington State Department of Ecology, to assess the potential effects of future population and water-use changes in the Chimacum Creek Basin and vicinity. The model was developed and calibrated for steady-state conditions to evaluate forecast population changes, full beneficial use of the Jefferson County Public Utility District #1 water rights, and conversion of septic systems to sanitary sewer system within the Urban Growth Area. The model also was used to evaluate the effects of groundwater withdrawals used for agriculture with respect to magnitude and depth of withdrawals. Particle tracking was used with the model to gain understanding of the locations of groundwater recharge with respect to the ultimate location of groundwater discharge. An analysis of model mass balances from many simulations with a single pumping well in different locations provided a map of the areal variation in response coefficients for the well, indicating the fraction of water being pumped by the well that resulted in lowered streamflow in Chimacum Creek.

A transient calibration of the groundwater-flow model was attempted as well, in order to assess the temporal aspects of the aquifer response to the changes in population and water use that were studied with the steady-state application of the model. The calibration was achieved only by allowing the solution of the numerical simulation to halt before satisfactory convergence of the products of the governing equations was attained. As such, the calibration of a transient version of the model was deemed inappropriate for use in assessing the temporal aspects of changes in stresses to the aquifer system.

Documentation of the attempt to calibrate a transient version of the steady-state model, however, was considered important, although not appropriate for inclusion in a report on the steady-state results. The range of variables considered, the magnitude of the differences between target calibration and simulated values, and possible approaches to achieve calibration that were not attempted could help future research efforts achieve success. This report is a supplement to Jones and others (2013) and presents the results of an attempt to calibrate a transient version of the Chimacum Creek groundwater-flow model.

Purpose and Scope

The purpose of this report is to present the results of an attempt to calibrate a transient version of the steady-state model calibrated for and reported on by Jones and others (2013). It summarizes parts of the construction and calibration of the steady-state model that are relevant to the transient calibration. This report references figures and tables included in Jones and others (2013) that are not reproduced here.

Description of Study Area

The model covers an area of about 64 mi^2 on the Olympic Peninsula in northeastern Jefferson County, Washington (fig. 1). The Chimacum Creek Basin drains an area of about 53 mi^2 and consists of Chimacum Creek and its tributary East Fork Chimacum Creek. These creeks converge near the town of Chimacum and discharge to Port Townsend Bay near the town of Irondale. The topography of the study area consists of narrow, regularly spaced parallel ridges and grooves that are characteristic of fluted glaciated surfaces; they are oriented in a north-south direction (Ritter, 1978). This surface has been incised locally by fluvial and postglacial erosion, producing steep sides and hummocky bottoms for the valley. Thick accumulations of peat occur along the axis of East Fork Chimacum Creek and provide rich, agriculturally productive soils. The study area is underlain by a north-thickening sequence of unconsolidated glacial and interglacial deposits. Sedimentary and igneous bedrock units underlie the unconsolidated deposits and crop out along the margins and the western interior of the study area.

The study area has a temperate marine climate with warm, dry summers, and cool, wet winters. Chimacum Creek Basin lies within the rain shadow of the Olympic Mountains, and the annual average precipitation during 1981–2010 at the community of Center (fig. 1) was 28.78 in/yr (National Oceanic and Atmospheric Administration, 2007). In 1996, the population of the Chimacum Creek Basin was 5,675 people, and is projected to increase by almost 30 percent by 2016 (Parametrix and others, 2000). Population density in the basin is highest near the mouth of Chimacum Creek, in the general area of Irondale, Port Hadlock, and Chimacum (fig. 1).

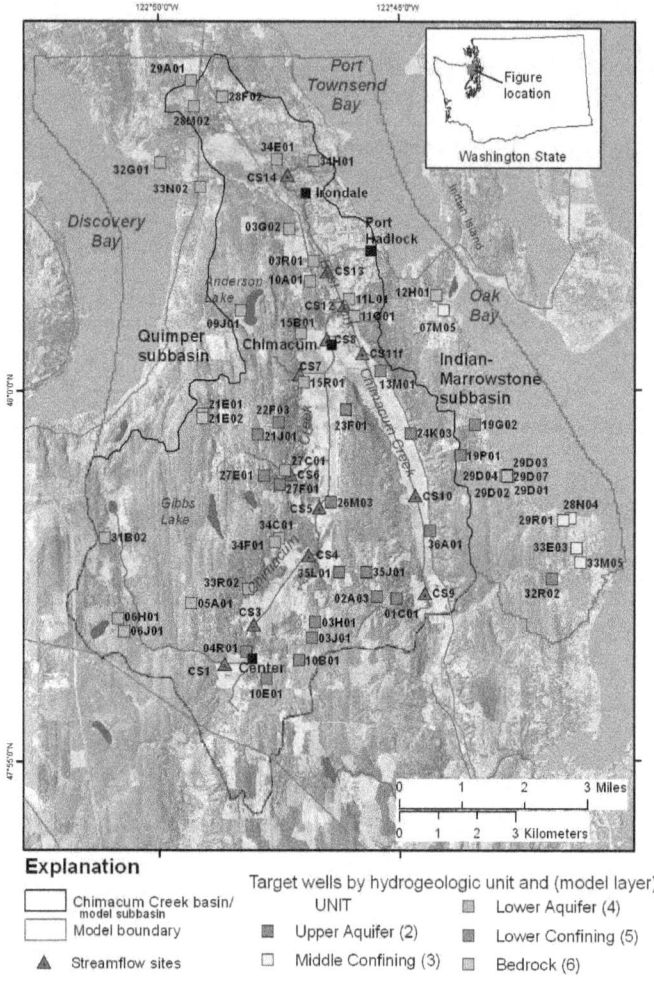

Figure 1. Map showing locations of surface-water measurements and wells used for calibration, Chimacum Creek Basin and vicinity, Jefferson County, Washington.

Groundwater-Flow System

The geologic setting for Chimacum Creek Basin and the adjacent lands to the west, bordering Discovery Bay, and to the east, bordering Port Townsend Bay and Oak Bay, are typical of the Puget Sound Lowlands; unconsolidated deposits of glacial and interglacial origin are present throughout the study area. A typical glacial sequence progresses from advance outwash, to till, to recessional outwash. Fluvial, lacustrine, bog, and marsh depositional environments were common during interglacial periods. The modern-day drainage pattern of Chimacum Creek is mostly determined by pre-existing drainage pathways established by Vashon recessional outwash channels.

As described in Jones and others (2011) and Jones and others (2013), aquifers consist primarily of coarse-grained glacial outwash, but they also may include coarse-grained sediments within glacial till and coarse-grained interglacial deposits. The hydrogeologic units representing aquifers are the Upper Aquifer unit (UA, model layer 2) and the Lower Aquifer unit (LA, model layer 4). The hydrogeologic units roughly correspond with geologic units recessional outwash (UA) and advance outwash (LA) of the Vashon glacial deposits. The Lower Confining unit (LC, model layer 5) is a productive aquifer in some places. In other places, hundreds of feet of clay make LC a confining unit. Because most wells are finished in UA and LA, there were insufficient data to credibly subdivide the LC interglacial deposits (and possibly deposits from pre-Vashon glacial epochs) into distinct geologic or hydrogeologic units. Confining units consist primarily of fine-grained glacial outwash, unsorted and compacted glacial till, glaciolacustrine deposits, and fine-grained interglacial deposits. The hydrogeologic units representing confining layers are the Upper Confining unit (UC, model layer 1) and the Middle Confining unit (MC, model layer 3). The Lower Confining (LC, model layer 5) is not distinctly a confining unit. UC roughly corresponds with geologic unit Quaternary alluvial, and MC roughly corresponds with Vashon till. Unconsolidated aquifer and confining units are underlain by low-permeability Eocene to Oligocene sedimentary and igneous bedrock (hydrogeologic unit Bedrock, OE, model layer 6). Jones and others (2013, figs. 1 and 4, table 1) are useful references for the orientation, extent, and composition of the aquifer and confining hydrogeologic units.

Recharge from precipitation is the dominant source of water to the aquifer system. Return flow (recharge resulting from water use) from irrigation and septic systems contribute small amounts of recharge. Discharge is primarily to marine waters below sea level and to Chimacum Creek and its tributaries. Springs, seeps, and wells for public supply, domestic supply, and agriculture comprise the balance of groundwater discharge. Historical and projected public-supply use of groundwater are shown in figure 2 and table 1. Jones and others (2013, fig. 3) shows the location and magnitude of recharge from precipitation; Jones and others (2013, table 3) provides estimates of the major components of the groundwater budget.

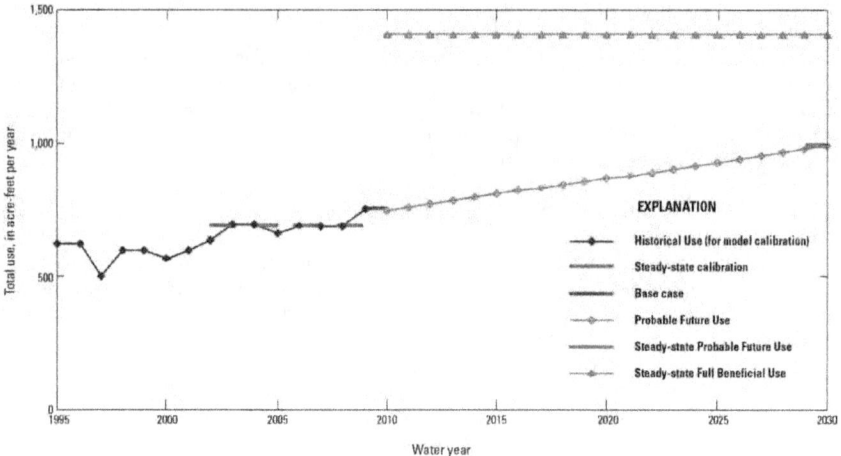

Figure 2. Graph showing historical groundwater use, Probable Future Use, steady-state Full Beneficial Use and total groundwater use for the Jefferson County Public Utility District #1, Chimacum Creek Basin and vicinity, Jefferson County, Washington, water years 1995–2030.

Table 1. Water use by residents within the Jefferson County Public Utility District #1 (public-supply use), and by residents and agriculture outside the public-supply area (self-supplied use); and the resultant recharge of groundwater by return flow from each class of user, during each year of the recorded period 1994–2009, Chimacum Creek Basin and vicinity, Jefferson County, Washington.

| | Source of usage or return flows, in acre-feet per year | | | | | | | | |
| | PUD | | | | | | Public | | |
Water year	Probable Use	Full Beneficial Use	Kala Point	Self-supplied	Irrigation	Precip-itation Recharge	water return (Probable Use)	Agri-culture return	Self-supplied return
1995	622	1,406	172	179	327	18,261	567	76	121
1996	622	1,406	175	182	327	18,391	569	76	123
1997	501	1,406	176	183	327	19,476	487	76	124
1998	601	1,406	179	186	327	20,323	550	76	126
1999	597	1,406	181	189	327	23,108	566	76	128
2000	570	1,406	184	191	327	13,332	532	76	129
2001	599	1,406	189	197	327	13,055	559	76	133
2002	637	1,406	193	200	327	12,084	583	76	135
2003	695	1,406	195	203	327	13,297	623	76	137
2004	695	1,406	198	205	327	13,015	630	76	139
2005	665	1,406	201	209	327	13,727	608	76	141
2006	691	1,406	206	214	327	19,283	627	76	145
2007	688	1,406	208	216	327	13,956	631	76	146
2008	688	1,406	210	218	327	10,717	634	76	147
2009	751	1,406	211	219	327	13,132	669	76	149
2010	748	1,406	213	220	327	15,456	667	76	149
2011	759	1,406	215	223	327	15,456	676	76	151
2012	771	1,406	218	226	327	15,456	686	76	153
2013	783	1,406	221	229	327	15,456	697	76	155
2014	796	1,406	224	232	327	15,456	707	76	157
2015	809	1,406	226	235	327	15,456	718	76	159
2016	821	1,406	229	238	327	15,456	729	76	161
2017	833	1,406	232	241	327	15,456	739	76	163
2018	844	1,406	235	243	327	15,456	748	76	165
2019	855	1,406	237	246	327	15,456	758	76	167
2020	866	1,406	240	249	327	15,456	767	76	168
2021	878	1,406	242	251	327	15,456	777	76	170
2022	889	1,406	245	254	327	15,456	787	76	172
2023	901	1,406	248	257	327	15,456	797	76	174
2024	913	1,406	250	260	327	15,456	807	76	176
2025	925	1,406	253	263	327	15,456	817	76	178
2026	937	1,406	256	266	327	15,456	828	76	180
2027	950	1,406	259	269	327	15,456	838	76	182
2028	962	1,406	262	271	327	15,456	849	76	184
2029	975	1,406	265	274	327	15,456	860	76	186
2030	988	1,406	267	277	327	15,456	871	76	188

Numerical Simulation of the Groundwater-Flow System

Groundwater flow in the Chimacum Creek Basin and vicinity was simulated using the U.S. Geological Survey modular three-dimensional finite-difference groundwater-flow model, MODFLOW-2005 (Harbaugh, 2005). The model described in detail in Jones and others (2013) was developed to simulate steady-state conditions. The model is comprised of a grid of 245 columns and 313 rows; cells are a uniform 200 ft per side. There are six model layers, each representing one hydrogeologic unit: (1) Upper Confining unit (UC); (2) Upper Aquifer unit (UA); (3) Middle Confining unit (MC); (4) Lower Aquifer unit (LA); (5) Lower Confining unit (LC); and (6) Bedrock unit (OE). The boundaries of the model coincide with natural topographic, geologic, and hydrologic boundaries except the northern edge, which was located as far north as possible without approaching more densely populated areas north of the study area. Three types of boundaries were used in the model: specified flux (recharge and pumping wells), head-dependent flux (constant head, general head, and drains), and no flow (outer model boundary) (Jones and others, 2013, fig. 3). The bottom boundary of the model is a no-flow boundary (bottom of layer 6 at an altitude of 1,500 ft below NAVD 88). The areal boundaries along the southern edge of the model correspond with the drainage basin boundaries of Chimacum Creek. These natural features act as no-flow boundaries as they are considered coincident with groundwater divides.

The steady-state simulation represented average conditions for October 1994–September 2009, which were used to calibrate the model. The steady-state calibration used as calibration targets average groundwater-level measurements in 57 wells (table 2), averaged surface-water baseflow measurements at 13 locations (table 3, streamgage 17B050 and 12 other synoptic baseflow measurement locations), plus estimated inflows to aquifer layers 2 and 4 through the northern boundary of the model. This calibration estimated the hydraulic conductivities of all layers, conductances for most boundary conditions, and preliminary stream conductances. For the transient calibration, groundwater levels were included for 37 of the wells and 119 surface-water flow measurements. The groundwater-level measurements were collected monthly during 2002–03 and 2008–09. The reported depth of the well screen and the well log were used to determine the model layer that represented the hydrogeologic unit screened by the well; for the small number of wells screened in multiple units, the unit with the larger screened interval was assigned. Surface-water baseflow measurements were collected at 13 locations (fig. 1) during three synoptic events (June and October 2002 and July 2007) that represent periods of low flow. Mean monthly baseflow values also were computed from the streamflow data measured at the gage 17B050 (CS14 in fig. 1) near the mouth of Chimacum Creek for October 2002–September 2009.

Table 2. Wells used in calibration, Chimacum Creek Basin and vicinity, Jefferson County, Washington.

[Location of wells shown in figure 1. N/A, not applicable]

Local well No.	Site identifier	Model layer	Number of measure-ments	Measured ground-water altitude (ft, NAVD 88)	Calibrated steady-state water level (ft, NAVD 88)	Steady-state residual (ft)	Mean of transient residuals (ft)	Standard deviation of transient residuals (ft)
28N/01W-01C01	475712122445901	5	1	265.77	255.34	10.43	12.55	N/A
28N/01W-02A03	475714122452401	5	2	273.17	268.34	4.83	7.77	0.31
28N/01W-03H01	475653122464101	5	1	279.16	273.72	5.44	10.09	N/A
28N/01W-03J01	475640122464501	5	1	286.21	277.80	8.41	13.31	N/A
28N/01W-04R01	475629122480701	2	15	205.56	200.67	4.89	1.76	0.59
28N/01W-05A01	475708122491501	4	1	284.35	273.87	10.48	16.00	N/A
28N/01W-06H01	475656122504501	4	2	385.29	382.42	2.87	9.43	0.04
28N/01W-06J01	475646122503801	4	2	377.69	377.14	0.55	7.46	0.08
28N/01W-10B01	475622122470101	5	2	294.07	298.74	-4.67	1.92	1.37
28N/01W-10E01	475608122474201	5	2	245.74	258.42	-12.68	-6.13	0.52
29N/01E-07M05	480106122440001	3	2	55.93	66.32	-10.39	-9.85	1.84
29N/01E-19G02	475933122432101	5	1	93.74	103.07	-9.33	-11.23	N/A
29N/01E-19P01	475908122433901	5	2	148.85	124.25	24.60	22.83	0.27
29N/01E-28N04	475816122412301	3	2	5.46	21.17	-15.71	-15.75	1.29
29N/01E-29D01	475852122424201	3	1	92.61	89.99	2.62	1.12	N/A
29N/01E-29D02	475851122424101	6	1	32.81	66.41	-33.60	-34.81	N/A
29N/01E-29D03	475852122424301	3	2	108.55	91.97	16.58	15.18	0.56
29N/01E-29D04	475851122424001	6	1	68.52	65.93	2.59	1.39	N/A
29N/01E-29D07	475851122424201	6	2	100.91	68.30	32.61	31.46	0.06
29N/01E-29R01	475815122413201	3	2	17.79	28.84	-11.05	-11.17	1.73
29N/01E-32R02	475728122414601	2	2	45.09	43.29	1.80	1.82	0.57
29N/01E-33E03	475752122411601	3	1	39.45	31.95	7.50	7.62	N/A
29N/01E-33M05	475741122411101	3	2	30.45	28.41	2.04	2.02	1.61
29N/01W-03G02	480211122471301	4	2	75.68	52.91	22.77	21.85	2.06
29N/01W-03R01	480145122464201	4	31	73.76	75.74	-1.98	1.20	1.19
29N/01W-09J01	480105122481401	4	1	287.43	287.26	0.17	-3.01	N/A
29N/01W-10A01	480129122464701	4	2	86.94	86.92	0.02	-0.75	0.35
29N/01W-11L01	480115122455701	4	2	105.36	96.75	8.61	7.73	0.55
29N/01W-11Q01	480101122455101	4	2	92.29	105.39	-13.10	-14.22	0.39
29N/01W-12H01	480118122440901	6	1	80.67	66.61	14.06	13.92	N/A
29N/01W-13M01	480016122451901	5	32	119.92	117.65	2.27	0.02	0.64
29N/01W-15B01	480047122465801	4	34	108.23	106.32	1.91	-0.07	1.04
29N/01W-15R01	480007122465301	4	34	127.85	124.27	3.58	-1.50	3.50
29N/01W-21E01	475942122490101	6	2	624.65	620.90	3.75	4.27	0.82
29N/01W-21E02	475938122490101	6	2	617.36	620.02	-2.66	-2.09	1.20
29N/01W-21J01	475925122475201	5	1	244.47	207.12	37.35	39.58	N/A
29N/01W-22F03	475935122472601	5	2	183.13	175.08	8.05	8.30	1.40

Local well No.	Site identifier	Model layer	Number of measure-ments	Measured ground-water altitude (ft, NAVD 88)	Calibrated steady-state water level (ft, NAVD 88)	Steady-state residual (ft)	Mean of transient residuals (ft)	Standard deviation of transient residuals (ft)
29N/01W-23F01	475945122460201	5	19	136.68	120.87	15.81	-3.89	1.82
29N/01W-24K03	475926122444101	5	35	132.33	124.18	8.15	-1.05	0.87
29N/01W-26M03	475830122462101	2	1	122.79	132.39	-9.60	-9.64	N/A
29N/01W-27C01	475856122471801	4	2	221.27	206.59	14.68	16.92	0.34
29N/01W-27E01	475851122474401	5	1	173.8	179.48	-5.68	-5.03	N/A
29N/01W-27F01	475844122472501	5	2	177.21	171.08	6.13	6.34	0.79
29N/01W-31B02	475802122510101	4	2	442.95	445.00	-2.05	3.01	0.38
29N/01W-33R02	475720122480401	4	2	248.26	254.57	-6.31	-1.65	0.68
29N/01W-34C01	475801122472601	4	2	185.61	204.76	-19.15	-16.73	0.59
29N/01W-34F01	475758122473001	4	2	242.07	213.03	29.04	31.81	0.33
29N/01W-35J01	475734122453701	5	32	276.41	270.01	6.40	0.22	0.73
29N/01W-35L01	475734122461101	5	1	276.76	262.80	13.96	15.92	N/A
29N/01W-36A01	475807122441701	5	1	150.41	138.65	11.76	10.66	N/A
30N/01W-28F02	480358122483501	4	2	165.56	112.48	53.08	52.94	0.27
30N/01W-28M02	480350122491001	4	2	124.3	116.62	7.68	7.60	0.91
30N/01W-29A01	480411122491501	4	1	141.85	120.45	21.40	21.33	N/A
30N/01W-32G01	480305122495201	4	1	2.69	36.38	-33.69	-33.74	N/A
30N/01W-33N02	480245122490201	4	1	38.95	23.70	15.25	14.57	N/A
30N/01W-34E01	480308122472801	4	1	78.2	38.51	39.69	38.36	N/A
30N/01W-34H01	480306122464201	4	2	8.2	24.66	-16.46	-18.11	0.59

Table 3. Flow measurement locations used for calibration, Chimacum Creek Basin and vicinity, Jefferson County, Washington.

Map ID (see fig. 1)	Site location	Number of measure-ments	Average flow measure-ment (ft^3/s)	Calibrated steady-state flow (ft^3/s)	Steady-state residual (ft^3/s)	Mean of transient residuals (ft^3/s)	Standard deviation of transient residual (ft^3/s)
CS1	Chimacum Creek, 20 ft upstream from sediment basin, and 0.8 mi west of Center	3	0.65	0.12	0.52	0.53	0.29
CS3	Chimacum Creek, 50 ft downstream from West Valley Road, and 0.6 mi northwest of Center.	3	2.50	2.52	-0.02	-0.06	0.32
CS4	Chimacum Creek, at Center Road bridge, and 1.7 mi north of Center	3	2.98	3.79	-0.81	-0.88	0.20
CS5	Chimacum Creek, 100 ft downstream from road bridge, and 2.4 mi north of Center.	3	4.08	5.15	-1.07	-1.15	0.47
CS6	Naylor Creek, 10 ft upstream from weir, 50 ft downstream from West Valley Road, and 2.8 mi north of Center	3	0.24	0.00	0.24	0.24	0.17
CS7	Putaansuu Creek, 10 ft downstream from West Valley Road, and 0.9 mi southwest of Chimacum	3	0.12	0.03	0.09	0.09	0.04
CS8	Chimacum Creek, at Rhody Drive bridge, and 0.3 mi west of Chimacum	3	3.70	4.73	-1.03	-1.52	1.14
CS9	East Fork Chimacum Creek, 30 ft upstream from Egg and I Road, and 2.0 mi north of Beaver Valley	3	0.67	0.03	0.64	0.64	0.06
CS10	East Fork Chimacum Creek, upstream from culvert, and 3.2 mi south of Chimacum	3	1.59	0.15	1.44	1.41	0.17
CS11f	East Fork Chimacum Creek, Beaver Valley Road, and 0.3 mi southeast of Chimacum	2	1.24	0.00	1.24	-1.08	1.07
CS12	East Fork Chimacum Creek, 20 ft downstream from Chimacum Road, and 0.6 mi north of Chimacum	3	1.21	0.08	1.13	-0.87	0.88
CS13	Chimacum Creek, at PUD gage, 50 ft upstream from footbridge, 300 ft east of end of Hilda Road, 1.2 mi north of Chimacum, and at mile 2.3	3	7.14	2.27	4.87	2.13	0.95
CS14	Chimacum Creek, 0.7 mi upstream from mouth	84	11.29	7.41	3.88	0.36	8.49

The sensitivity of the simulated model output to changes in the parameter value determines the uncertainty of the estimated parameter values; values are better estimated for parameters with a high sensitivity (a large effect on simulated head). In contrast, changing the value of parameters with low sensitivity has little effect on the model-calibration process and values for these insensitive parameters are not well estimated.

Values for 189 parameters (that is, pilot points for horizontal and vertical hydraulic conductivities, and conductances for general head, drain, and stream boundary conditions) were computed in the steady-state calibration. Sensitivities for these parameters were calculated using an "identifiability" measure that is included in the PEST procedure (Doherty and Hunt, 2009) based on "singular values" and associated vectors that are part of the Singular Value Decomposition Assist (SVDA) procedure. These vectors relate each parameter to its influence on the objective function; that is the sum of squared weighted errors at all target wells and streamflow targets. The resulting identifiability values (square root of the sum of the vector components for a given parameter) are shown in Jones and others (2013, fig. 9). The model is most sensitive to horizontal conductivities (Kx) in layers 2, 4, and 6 with pilot points in the central portion of these units being best identified (>75 percent identifiability) as seen by the high values on the left of the Kx2, Kx4, and Kx6 portions of Jones and others (2013, fig. 9).

The results of the steady-state calibration were assessed by comparing simulated and measured groundwater levels and stream baseflows, and by examining the mean and standard errors of residuals (difference between measured and simulated values). The minimum standard error on the mean between simulated and measured groundwater levels (2.8 ft) based on standard error occurred in model layer 5 (Lower Confining unit LC); the maximum standard error (8.9 ft) occurred in model layer 6 (Bedrock unit, OE). Model layers 2 and 3 (UA and MC) had the lowest absolute value of mean residuals, indicating simulated groundwater levels in these units had the lowest model bias (Jones and others, 2013, table 7). Simulated steady-state groundwater-level altitudes in UA indicate flow generally moving down the valleys to the north from the drainage divide. Simulated steady-state groundwater-level altitudes in LA indicate flow generally moving down valley from the drainage divide to discharge in Discovery Bay, Port Townsend Bay, and Oak Bay. A groundwater divide occurs midway between Discovery Bay and Port Townsend Bay. Simulated steady-state groundwater-level altitudes in LC indicate flow generally moving down valley from the drainage divide toward the groundwater divide that occurs midway between Discovery Bay and Port Townsend Bay.

Baseflow discharge is reasonably well simulated by the steady-state calibration except for the East Fork Chimacum Creek. On average, the model underpredicts the amount of baseflow in the East Fork of Chimacum Creek and at two locations downstream of the confluence between Chimacum Creek and the East Fork (sites CS13 and CS14). This is likely due to the humic bogs present along the East Fork (locally known as "Magical Dirt"), which drain slowly giving the recession curve a logarithmic shape similar to one affected by large amounts of bank storage. This is evidenced by the dark brown color of the water in the reach during the summer months as the humic bogs slowly discharge to the creek.

Transient Calibration

Transient groundwater flow represents a dynamic system, in which variable inflows, outflows, and groundwater storage change with time. A calibration to transient conditions was performed which incorporated monthly variations in recharge and discharge. Transient conditions for calibration were simulated for October 1994–September 2009 using 180 monthly stress periods. During model calibration, variables were adjusted within probable ranges to minimize differences between measured and simulated groundwater levels and stream baseflows. The transient version of the model proved inherently unstable and was not used to simulate alternate hydrologic or anthropogenic changes.

The model was calibrated in a two-step process, first using steady-state simulations to estimate hydraulic conductivities of the six model layers to match measured heads and flows at target wells and streamflow sites, then using a transient simulation to estimate the parameters that predominantly affect fluctuations in flow, storage coefficients, and stream conductance. Calibrated values from the steady-state analysis were then used in attempts to calibrate the model using transient conditions, which included adjusting stream conductances and storage coefficients. Each transient stress period consists of three timesteps. Calibration of the transient simulation yielded estimates of storage coefficients in the upper layers, and estimates for stream conductance.

All model layers were simulated as confined units so that the transmissivity of each cell remained constant throughout the duration of the simulation. This simplification improved the numerical stability of the model. Although model layers 1–3 were simulated as confined, they are in reality largely unconfined, therefore, during the calibration process, storage coefficients were allowed to be as high as 0.5, to allow values that would be representative of specific yield values. Where model layers were conceptually confined, storage coefficients were assigned the value of $2.0(10)^{-6}$ ft^{-1}.

The initial time step in this transient analysis was based on a steady-state condition that simulates average recharge, discharge, and groundwater levels for predevelopment conditions (no anthropogenic development). The transient simulation period (October 1994–September 2009) was divided into 180 monthly stress periods to represent temporal variations in recharge, discharge, and storage. Agricultural groundwater withdrawals were apportioned between May and September, as was done for the surface-water diversions. Attempts to calibrate the transient model used head and flow data measured from October 2001 through September 2009 to estimate storage coefficients for (conceptually) unconfined model layers, and stream conductances for 33 stream reaches.

The model calibration used nonlinear regression with the parameter-estimation program PEST, with regularized inversion (Doherty, 2003, 2005), pilot points to represent heterogeneity of aquifer and confining unit properties, and SVDA. This approach allowed a relatively large number of parameters (189 parameters for the steady-state calibration and 97 for the transient case) to be estimated using a set of pilot points distributed throughout the model domain (Doherty, 2003, 2005). Hydraulic properties of each hydrogeologic unit within the model were then estimated through spatial interpolation using kriging from the pilot points to the model grid cells. The result is a smooth variation of the hydraulic property values within the model domain.

A number of studies have described the use of pilot points for groundwater-model calibration. Twenty-six pilot point locations were evenly spread throughout the model domain and were distributed vertically so that each hydrogeologic unit contained pilot points. Pilot points were not specified where a hydrogeologic unit was absent. Twenty pilot points were used for both hydraulic conductivity and storage coefficients with the remaining six pilot point locations added to estimate storage coefficients. Because not all pilot point locations had all hydrogeologic units present, it resulted in 150 active hydraulic conductivity pilot points (75 for Kx and 75 for Kz) and 32 pilot points for storage coefficients for (conceptually) unconfined conditions (see Jones and others, 2013, fig. 8).

The final values for calibration parameters are listed in table 4 and the areal distribution of horizontal and vertical conductivities are shown in Jones and others (2013, fig. 8A-L). The properties of layer 2 (Upper Aquifer unit, UA) are the dominant variables (vertical and horizontal hydraulic conductivity) and the properties of model layer 4 (Lower Aquifer unit, LA) are similarly significant. Model layers 1 (Upper Confining unit, UC) and 3 (Middle Confining unit, MC) have the highest values of storage coefficients (fig. 3A-F).

Table 4. Final values for calibration parameters.

Kh (ft/d)

Model layer	Number of active cells	Geomean	Minimum	Maximum	Change from initial estimate	Median thickness (ft)
1	3,136	0.375	0.002	32.04	× 0.38	30
2	9,150	167.6	0.436	498.8	× 10.1	<5
3	25,035	0.396	0.001	47.62	× 0.49	51
4	21,795	1.627	0.01	489.6	× 0.48	62
5	28,966	0.152	$1.0(10)^{-5}$	103.0	× 0.06	274
6	44,775	0.08	$7.0(10)^{-6}$	10.9	× 0.42	1,476

Kv (ft/d)

Model layer	Geomean	Minimum	Maximum	Change from initial estimate
1	6.27	4.04	10	× 1.13
2	17.9	0.427	50	× 0.69
3	0.184	$7.6(10)^{-5}$	4.94	× 0.64
4	6.69	0.751	43.3	× 0.64
5	0.73	$5.5(10)^{-5}$	10	× 0.71
6	0.165	$4.9(10)^{-4}$	0.977	× 1.37

Specific Storage (1/ft), for cells with unconfined conditions

Model layer	Number of cells with unconfined conditions	Geomean	Minimum	Maximum	Change from initial estimate
1	3,136	0.0563	0.0343	0.13	× 0.28
2	6,273	0.124	0.0497	0.20	× 0.62
3	24,839	0.159	0.0561	0.49	× 0.79
4	3,350	0.122	0.099	0.14	$× 1.0(10)^{5}$
5	9,088	0.111	0.044	0.33	$× 1.0(10)^{5}$
6	7,712	0.0482	0.0134	0.078	$× 4.8(10)^{4}$

Note: All cells with confined conditions were set at specific storage of $2.0(10)^{-6}$.

Drain Conductance (ft^2/d)

Drain group	Application	Final value	Change from initial estimate
0	Small streams, shallow bedrock	1,000	× 0.043
1	Coastal seeps	25,852	× 1.63

Table 4. Final values for calibration parameters.—Continued

GHB Conductance (ft²/d)

GHB group	Application	Final value	Change from initial estimate
0	Model boundaries in Puget Sound	907.7	× 0.00087
1	Lakes	$5.34(10)^8$	× 28.6
2	North boundary in Unit 2	100	Not in previous model
4	North boundary in Unit 4	$1.532(10)^5$	Not in previous model

Stream Conductance (ft²/d)

Stream reach	Final value	Change from initial estimate
1	3.2	× 0.298
2	66.0	× 0.207
3	763	× 77.2
4	96,612	× 764
5	0.37	× 0.0148
6	1,140	× 0.170
7	0.36	× 0.0006
9	0.87	× 0.0044
11	3,769	× 1.261
12	389	× 6.83
14	378,883	× 22.8
15	2,028	× 41.1
16	10.2	× 0.494
17	2.61	× 1.208
19	3,311	× 22.1
20	330	× 3.33
22	145	× 6.71
23	110.7	× 4.18
24	529	× 2.90
25	2,881	× 10.15
26	66,233	× 4.02
27	55.2	× 8.07
28	74.7	× 0.109
29	14.6	× 5.38
31	56,467	× 216
32	53.3	× 0.569
34	270,211	× 143.7
35	23,717	× 28.3
37	6,543	× 148.7
38	711	× 7.61
39	15,439	× 13.17
40	11,589	× 178.3
41	8.77	× 0.481

16

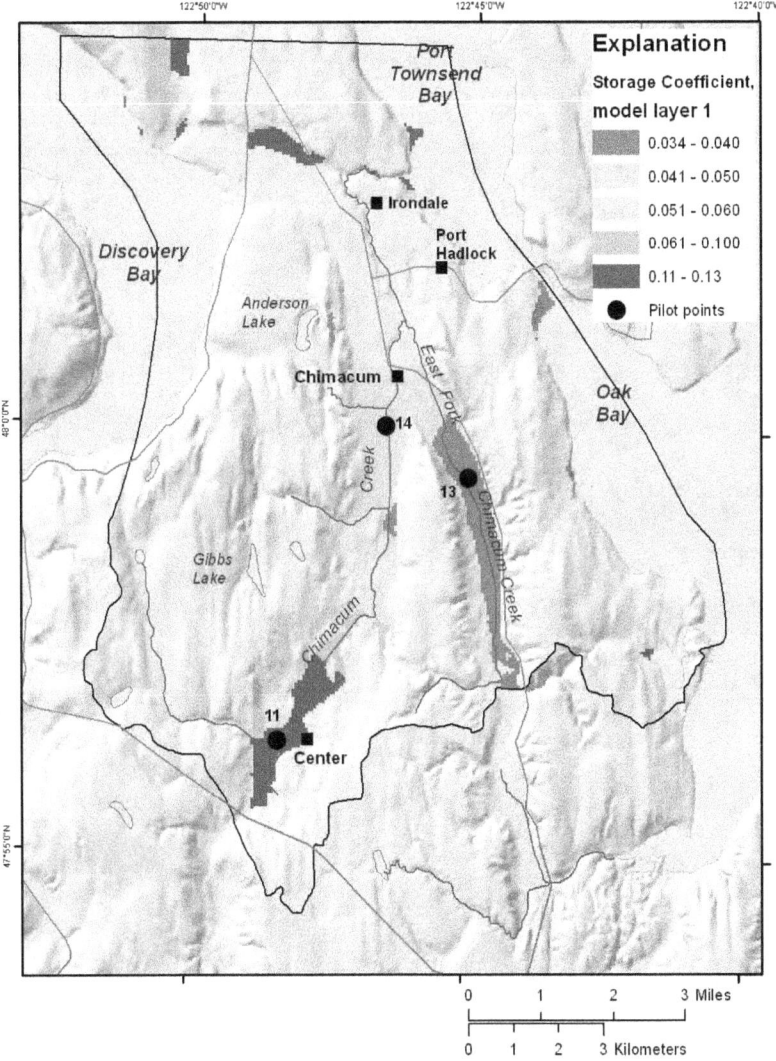

A. Layer 1; Upper Confining unit (UC).

Figure 3. Maps showing areal distribution of storage coefficient values, with shading indicating where the storage coefficient is specified as confined, and locations of storage coefficient calibration pilot points-for all model layers, Chimacum Creek Basin and vicinity, Jefferson County, Washington.

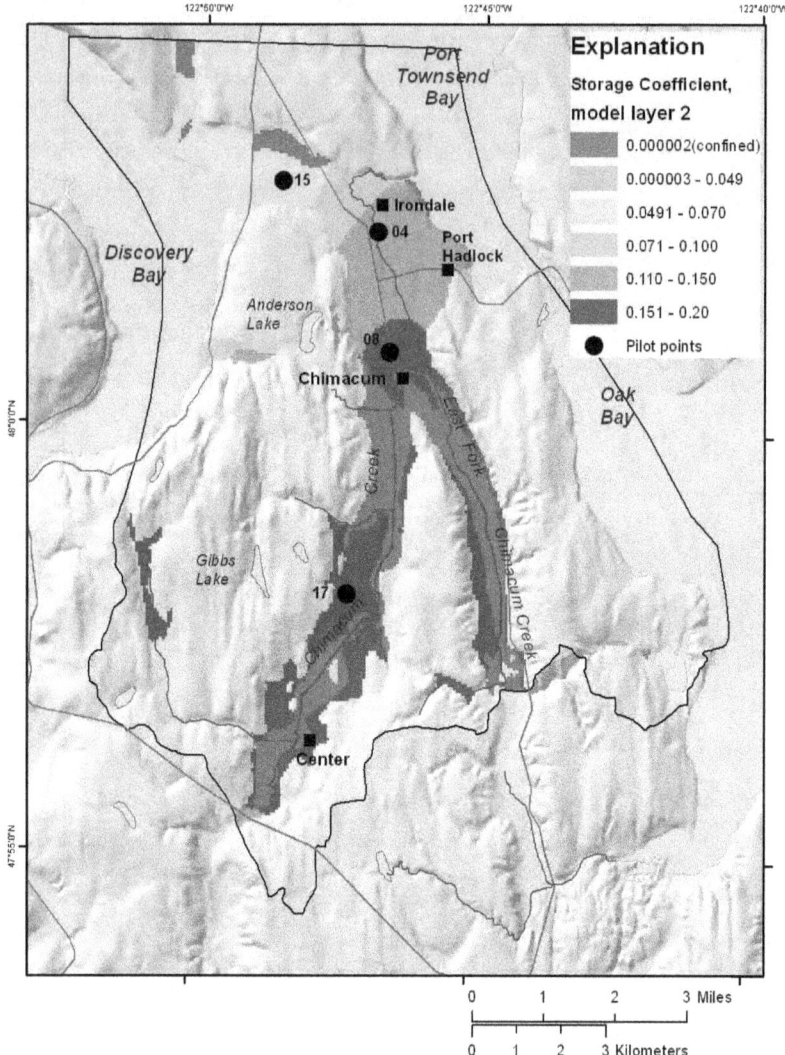

B. Layer 2; Upper Aquifer unit (UA).

Figure 3.—Continued.

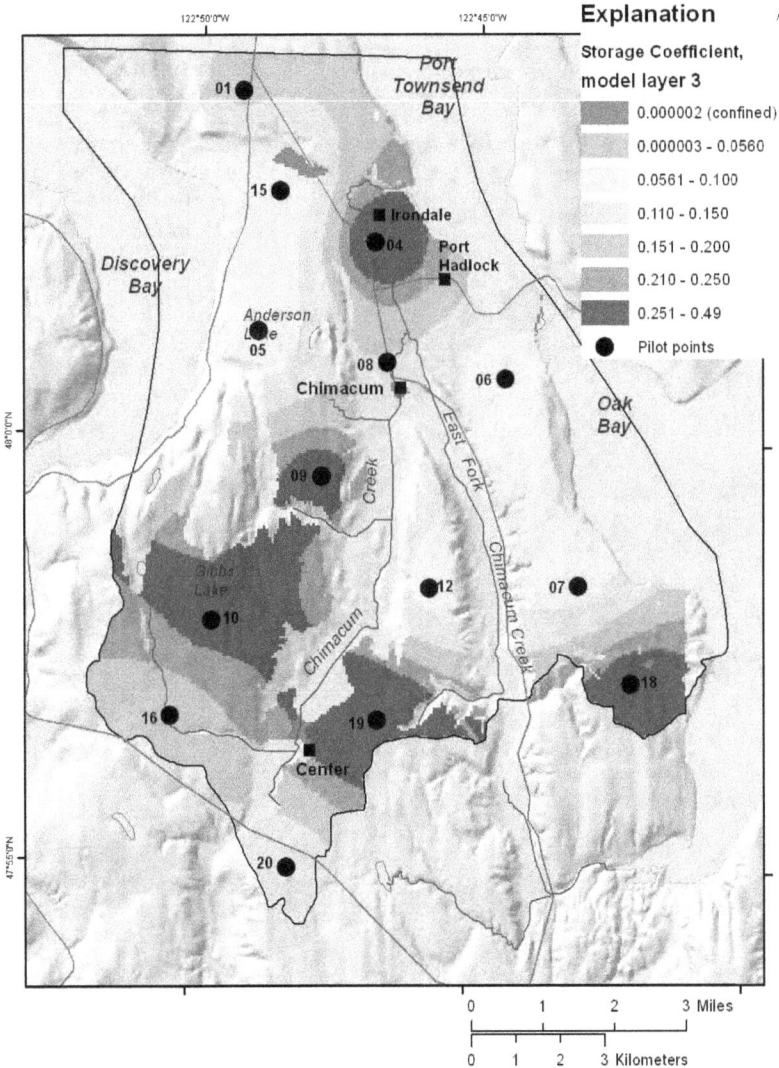

Explanation

Storage Coefficient, model layer 3

- 0.000002 (confined)
- 0.000003 - 0.0560
- 0.0561 - 0.100
- 0.110 - 0.150
- 0.151 - 0.200
- 0.210 - 0.250
- 0.251 - 0.49
- ● Pilot points

0   1   2   3 Miles

0   1   2   3 Kilometers

C. Layer 3; Middle Confining unit (MC).

Figure 3.—Continued.

19

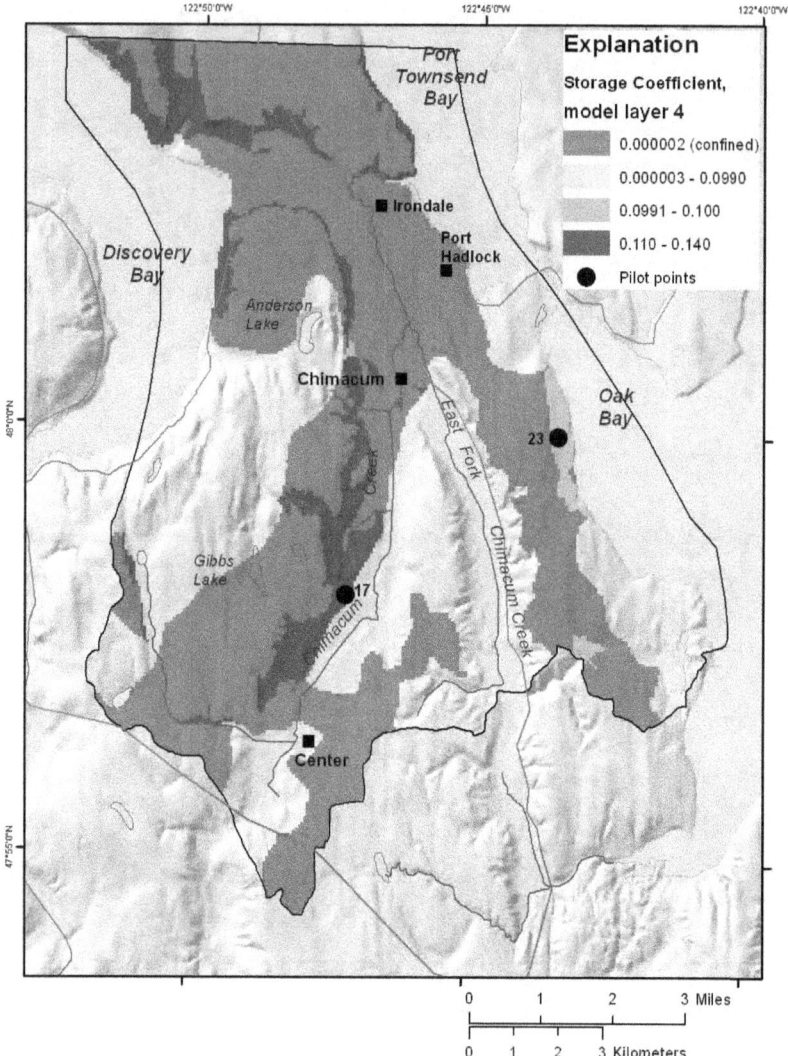

D. Layer 4; Lower Aquifer unit (LA).

Figure 3.—Continued.

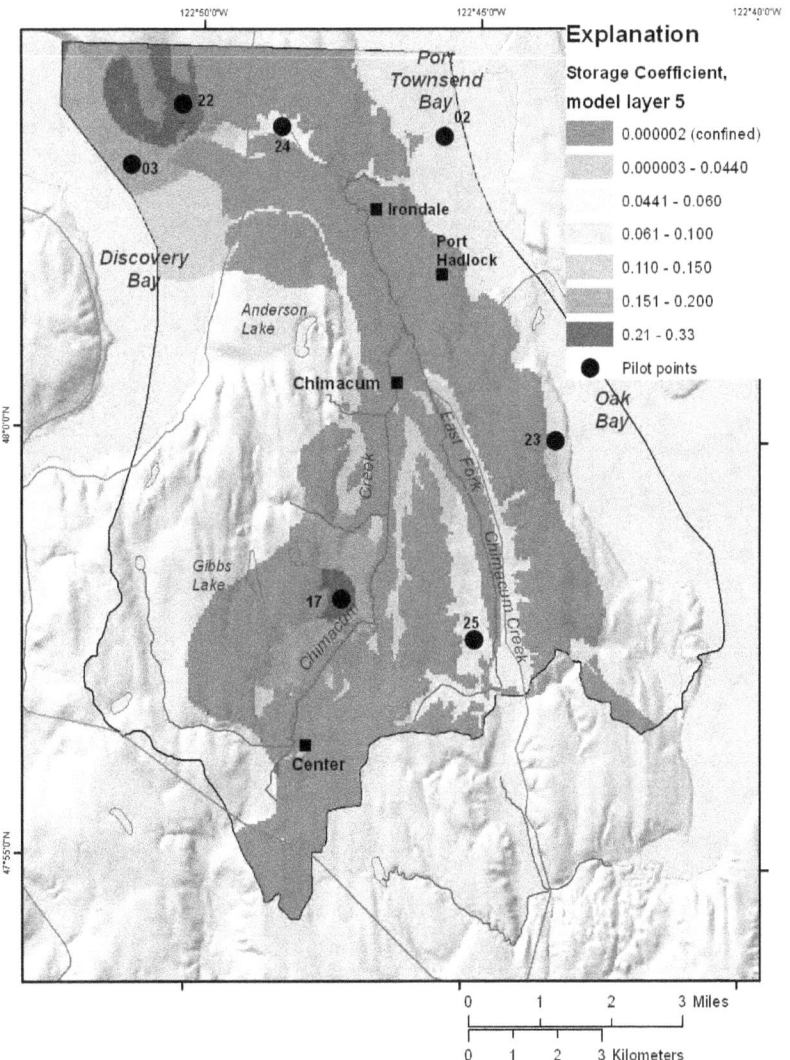

Explanation

Storage Coefficient, model layer 5

- 0.000002 (confined)
- 0.000003 - 0.0440
- 0.0441 - 0.060
- 0.061 - 0.100
- 0.110 - 0.150
- 0.151 - 0.200
- 0.21 - 0.33
- ● Pilot points

E. Layer 5; Lower Confining unit (LC)

Figure 3.—Continued.

21

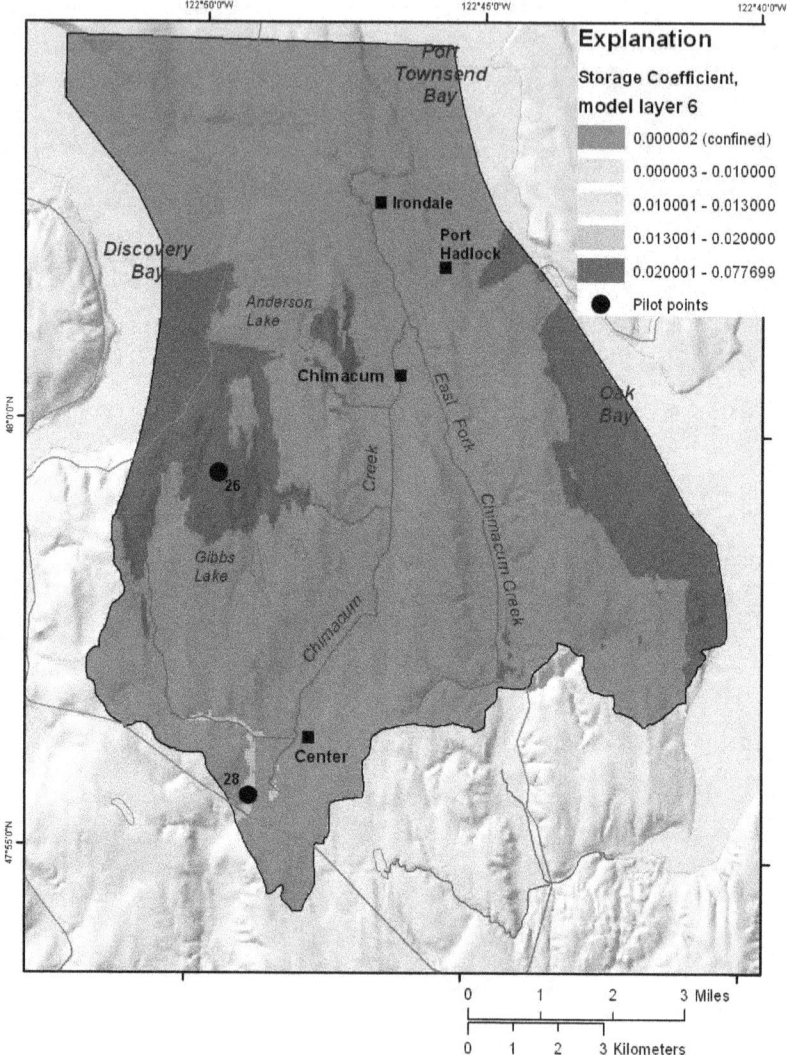

F. Layer 6; Bedrock unit (OE).

Figure 3.—Continued.

The transient calibration was complicated by persistent instability problems apparently caused by large variations in groundwater exchange with surface water between iterations of the solver. This resulted in long execution times and elevated residual estimates. The transient model proved inherently unstable. Due to temporal transitions from gaining reaches (groundwater discharging to the stream) to losing reaches (surface water recharging the aquifer), the model would not converge for any timestep, and could only be calibrated using a solution algorithm (pcgN) that would allow for non-convergence at any particular timestep and proceed to the next. No timesteps converged.

Calibrated groundwater level altitudes in the target wells agree on average with their measured values in a similar fashion to what was seen in the results of the steady-state calibration (fig. 4, table 5). The model as calibrated to transient conditions has a mean residual and standard error of 0.06 ft ± 0.45 ft for heads and 0.48 ± 0.06 ft^3/s for flows. The mean and standard errors of the mean residuals are smaller in magnitude (less than 1 ft) for all layers except in MC and OE, as well as overall, lower than those from the steady-state calibration and scaled by the range of measured values, the standard errors for all model layers (except model layer 3, MC) were less than 3 percent.

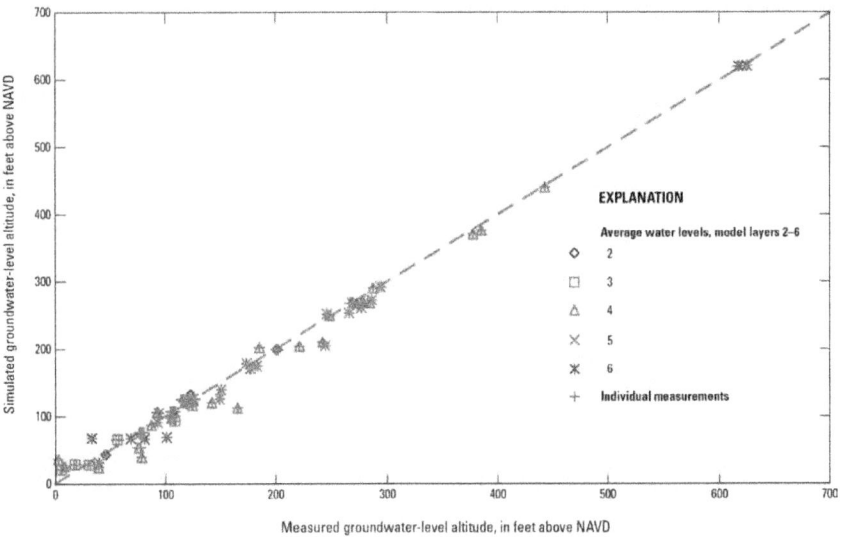

Figure 4. Graph showing simulated and measured groundwater-level altitudes for the calibrated model for transient conditions, Chimacum Creek Basin and vicinity, Jefferson County, Washington.

Table 5. Calibration statistics for the transient calibration by hydrogeologic unit and baseflow, Chimacum Creek Basin and vicinity, Jefferson County, Washington.

[**Abbreviations**: ft, feet; ft², square feet; NA, not applicable]

Hydrogeologic unit observation group	Count of observations	Mean of residuals (ft)	Standard error of residuals (ft)	Mean of absolute values of residuals (ft)	Objective function (sum of squared residuals) (ft²)	Range of measured values (ft)	Standard error of residual / Range of observations (percent)
Heads in UC (model layer 1)	0						
Heads in UA (model layer 2)	18	1.13	0.65	2.20	151	44.66 – 202.25	0.4
Heads in MC (model layer 3)	10	-3.91	3.75	10.79	1,420	4.50 – 109.05	3.6
Heads in LA (model layer 4)	133	1.89	0.92	5.22	15,477	2.69 – 443.17	0.2
Heads in LC (model layer 5)	140	0.52	0.48	2.72	4,493	39.45 – 295.04	0.2
Heads in OE (model layer 6)	9	5.31	6.65	13.97	3,434	32.81 – 625.23	1.1
Total: All heads	310	1.16	0.50	4.35	24,975	2.69 – 625.23	0.1
Baseflow observations, in cubic feet per second	119	0.23 (ft³/s)	0.66 (ft³/s)	4.56 (ft³/s)	6047 (ft³/s)²	0.1 – 44.4 (ft³/s)	1.5

Observed fluctuations are small (mostly 2 ft, but range from 0.5 to 9 ft) compared to the value of the average groundwater level (due to altitude and flow gradients), so variations are not obvious in the scatter plot (fig. 4). The hydrographs (figs. 5A and 5B) do show simulated fluctuations in groundwater level, but these fluctuations were not reproduced in the transient calibration to the magnitude shown in the measured values. To show the fluctuations in groundwater levels more clearly in the hydrographs, the scale for the simulated data (left axis) are shifted relative to the measured data (right axis) but both are shown to the same scale.

Simulated groundwater levels show the expected seasonal trend—higher groundwater levels in the late winter to lowest levels in the late summer in the few wells with sufficient measurements (for example, fig. 5B, wells 29N/01W-03R01 and 29N/01W-15R01, both in LA; and wells 29N/01W-13M01, 29N/01W-23F01, and 29N/01W-24K03, all in LC). There also is a multi-year fluctuation in a few wells with high groundwater levels in about 1999, and again in about 2006. The highest annual precipitation recorded at the NWS station Chimacum 4 S during the calibration period (1995–2009) were in 1999 (43.31 in.) and 2006 (35.29 in.).

The transient calibration also attempted to fit the baseflow measurements in the Chimacum Creek system. The standard deviation of the 119 observations was about 1.5 percent of the range of measurements (table 5). A comparison between simulated and measured streamflows are shown in figure 6. The highest simulated flows are 33 percent of the measured flows at the most downstream site (CS14). Low flows were less well estimated. Hydrographs for the measurements and simulations are shown in figure 7. The more upstream locations show the same simulated seasonal fluctuation that reflects groundwater level seasonal fluctuations—it can be seen in the measured flow but only at the gage where the most data are available (site CS14). However, also apparent in the flow hydrographs for the downstream sites (CS11f, CS12, CS13, and CS14) is a fluctuation that reflects the problematic instability of the transient model. These instabilities can be shown to arise in the cells near CS11f, downstream of the largest diversion.

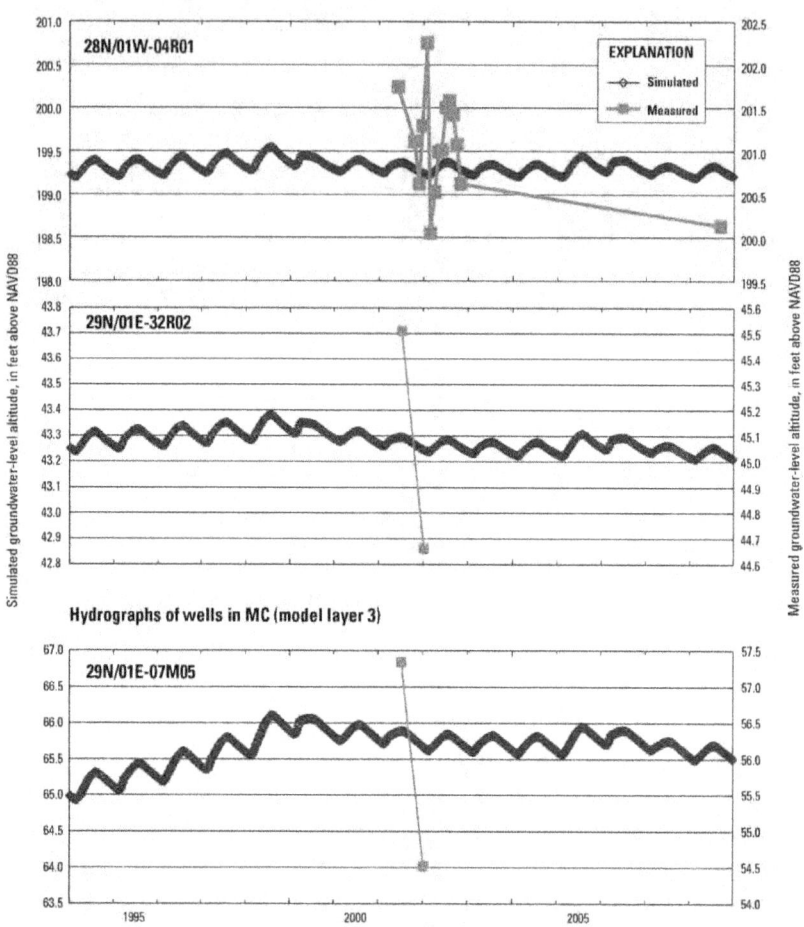

Figure 5. Hydrographs (*A*) and expanded hydrographs for selected wells (*B*) of simulated and measured groundwater-level altitudes for the calibrated model for transient conditions, Chimacum Creek Basin and vicinity, Jefferson County, Washington.

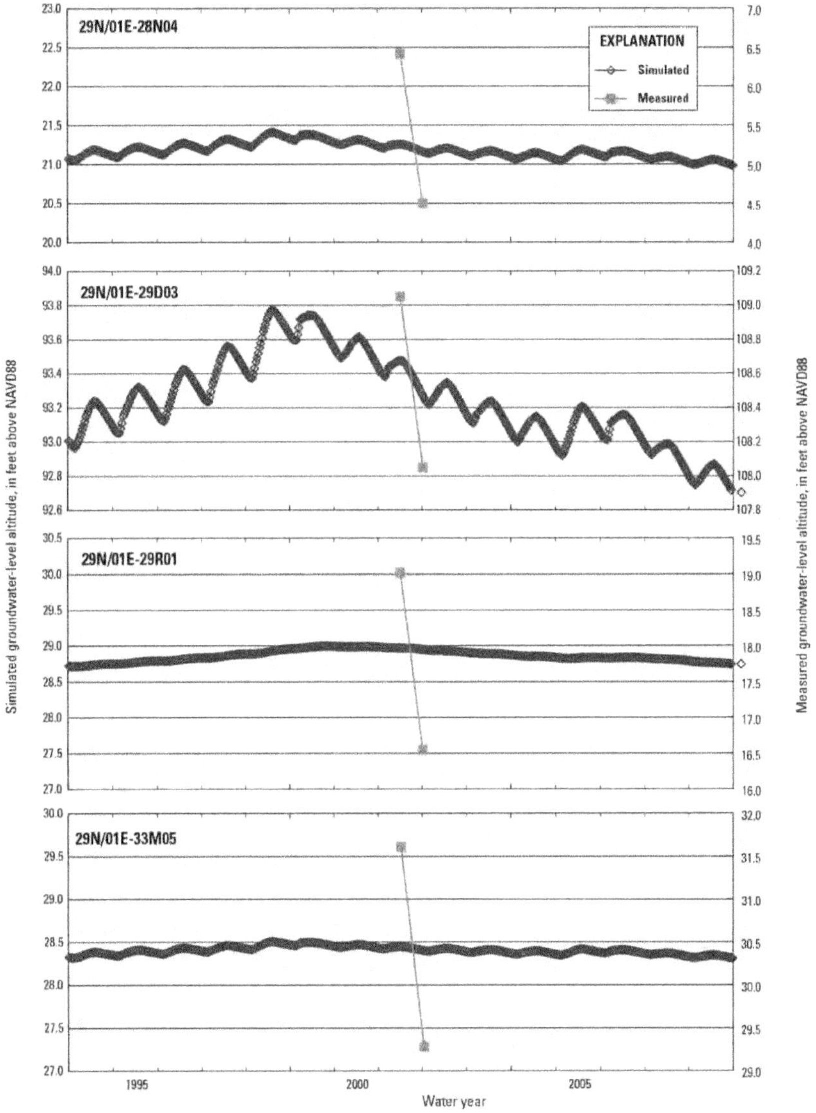

Figure 5A.—Continued.

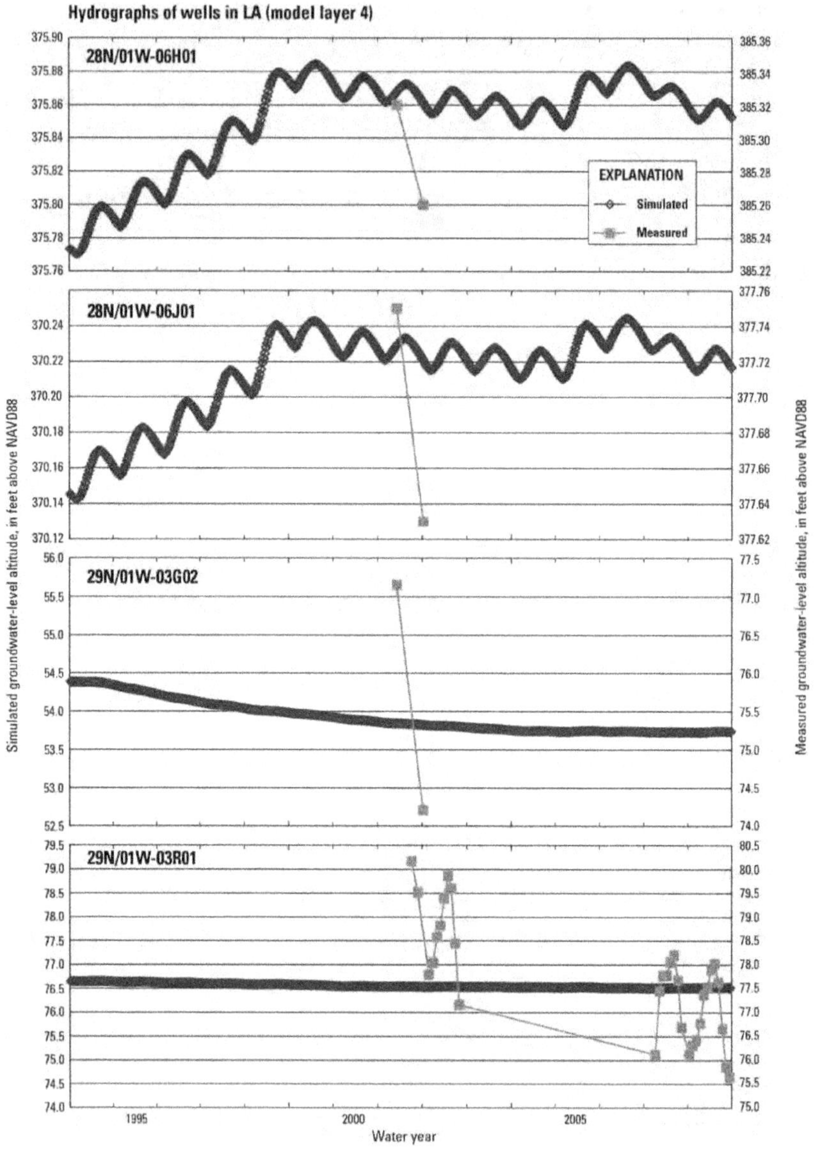

Hydrographs of wells in LA (model layer 4)

Figure 5A.—Continued.

Hydrographs of wells in LA (model layer 4)—Continued

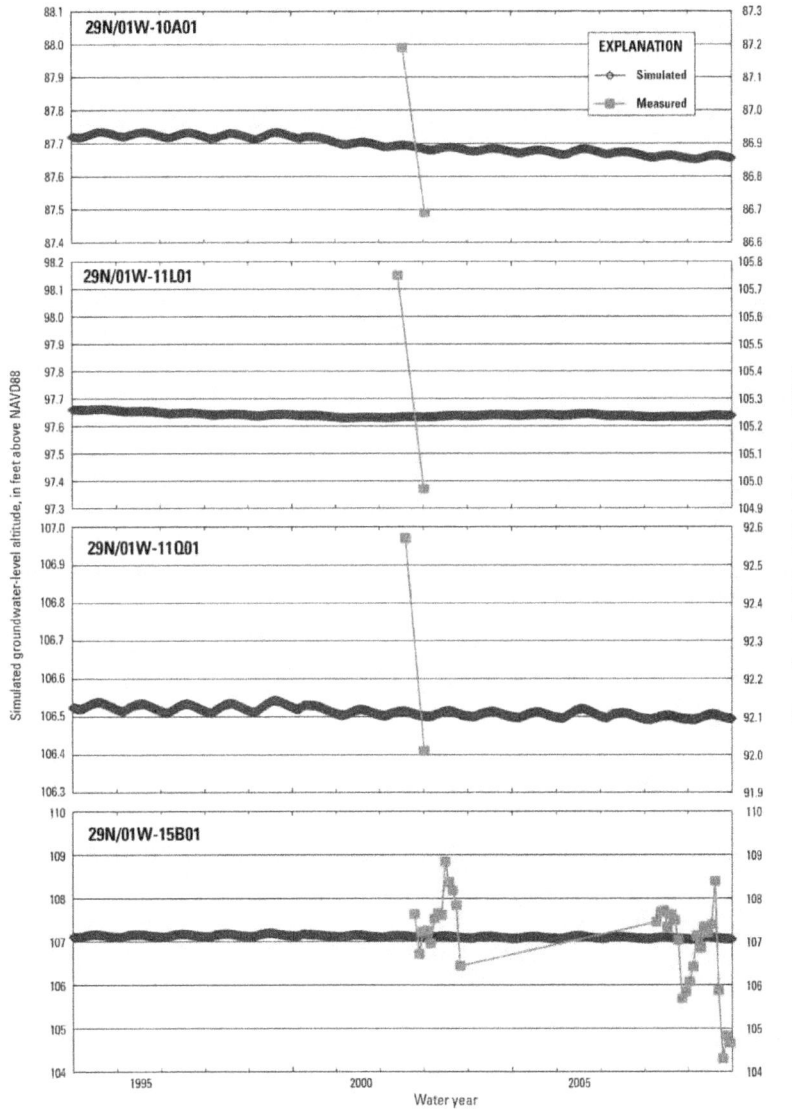

Figure 5A.—Continued.

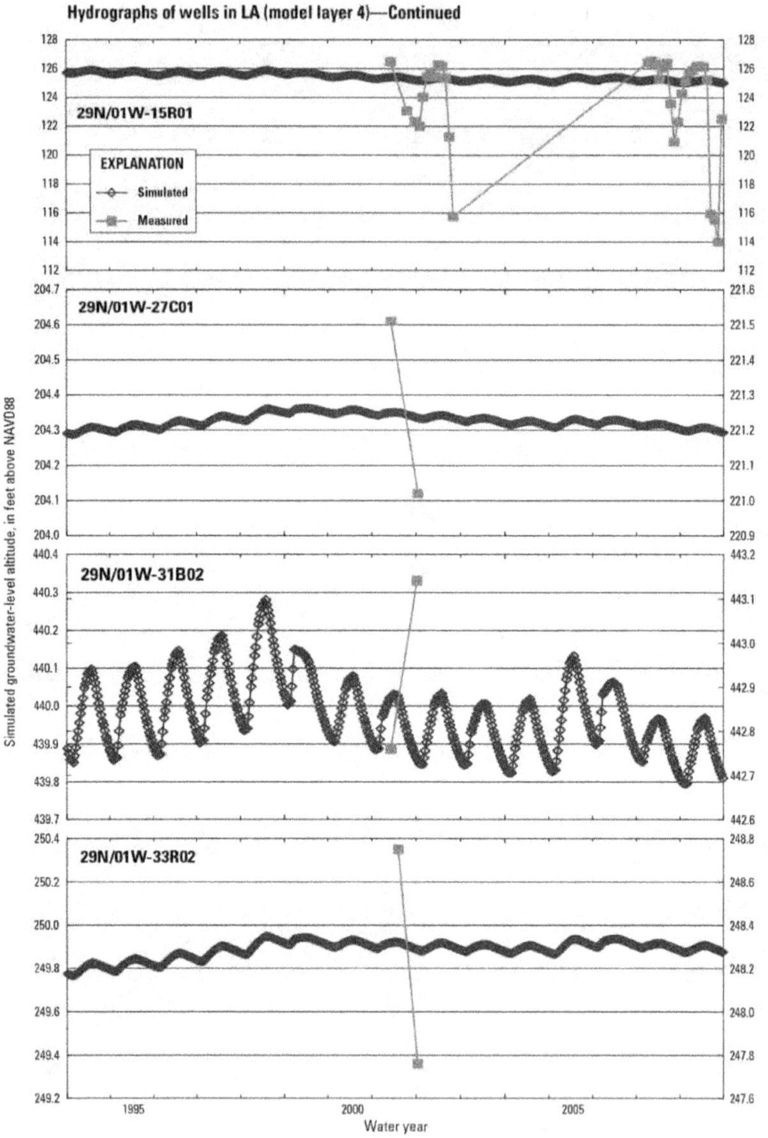

Hydrographs of wells in LA (model layer 4)—Continued
29N/01W-15R01
EXPLANATION
Simulated
Measured
29N/01W-27C01
29N/01W-31B02
29N/01W-33R02
Simulated groundwater-level altitude, in feet above NAVD88
Measured groundwater-level altitude, in feet above NAVD88
1995
2000
2005
Water year

Figure 5*A*.—Continued.

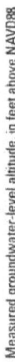

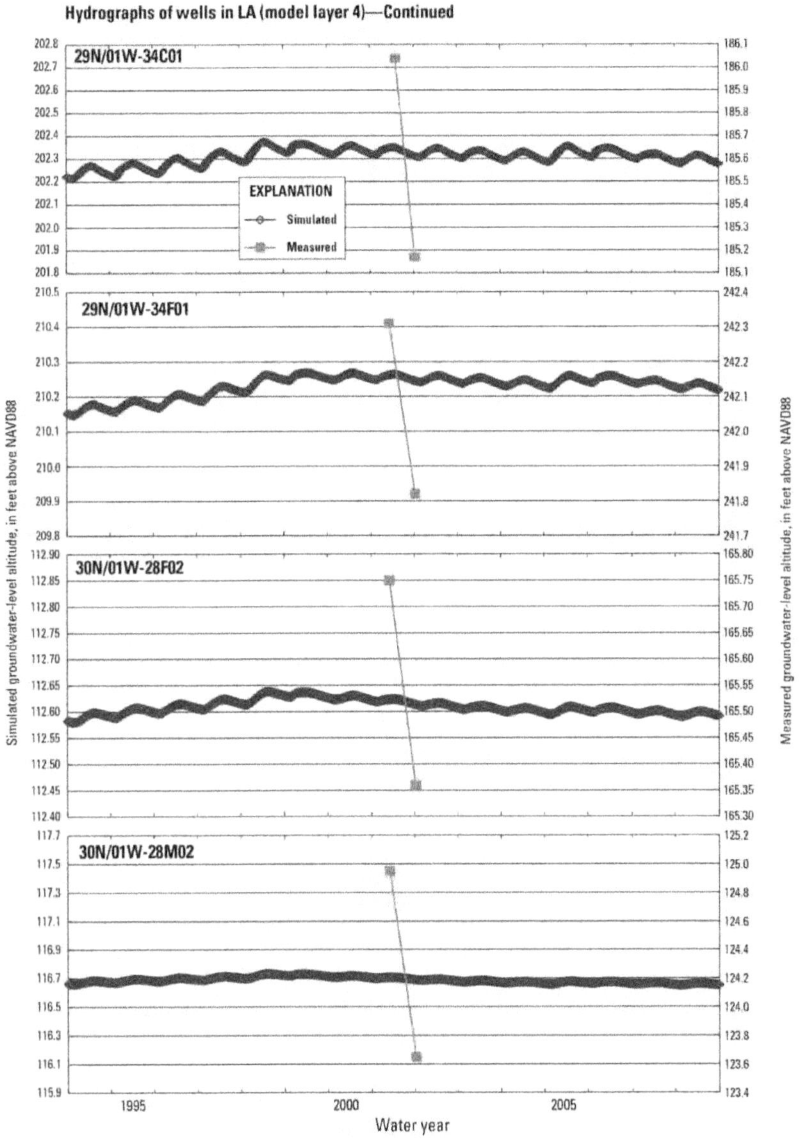

EXPLANATION
- ⊙— Simulated
- ▣— Measured

29N/01W-34C01

29N/01W-34F01

30N/01W-28F02

30N/01W-28M02

Simulated groundwater-level altitude, in feet above NAVD88

Measured groundwater-level altitude, in feet above NAVD88

Water year

Figure 5*A*.—Continued.

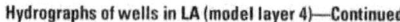

Hydrographs of wells in LA (model layer 4)—Continued

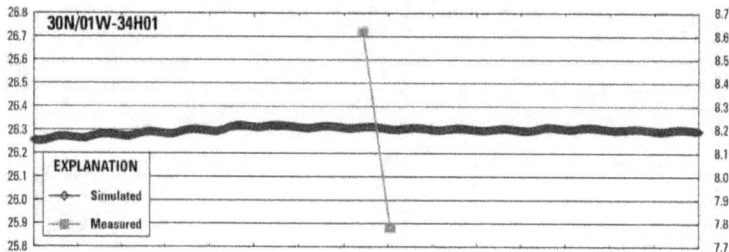

Hydrographs of Wells in LC (model layer 5)

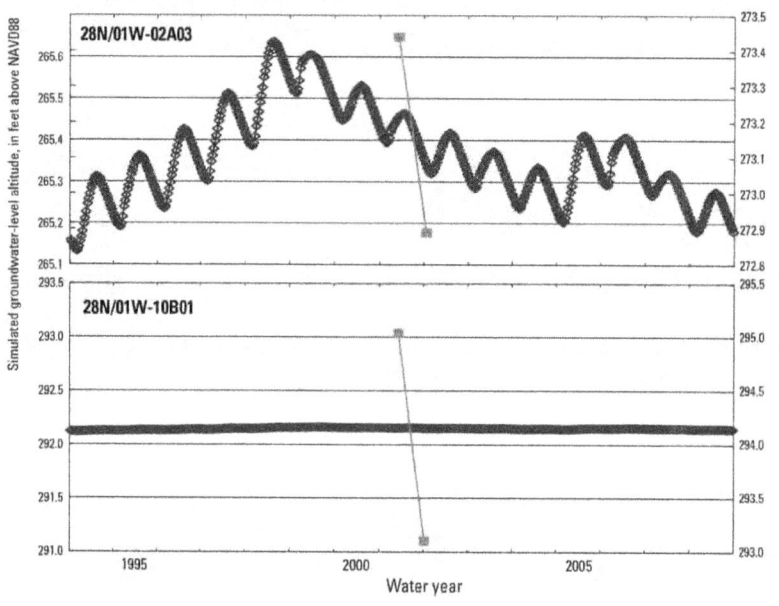

Water year

Figure 5A.—Continued.

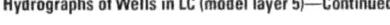

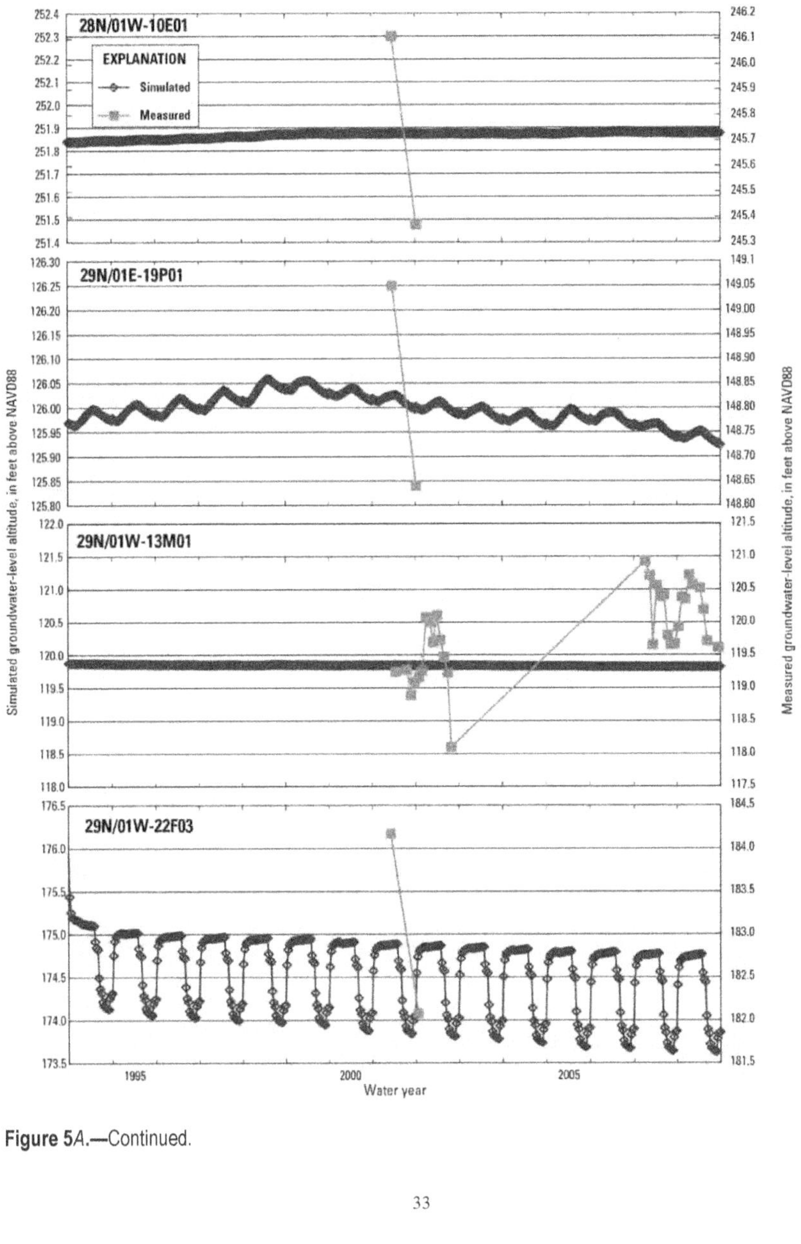

Figure 5A.—Continued.

Hydrographs of Wells in LC (model layer 5)—Continued

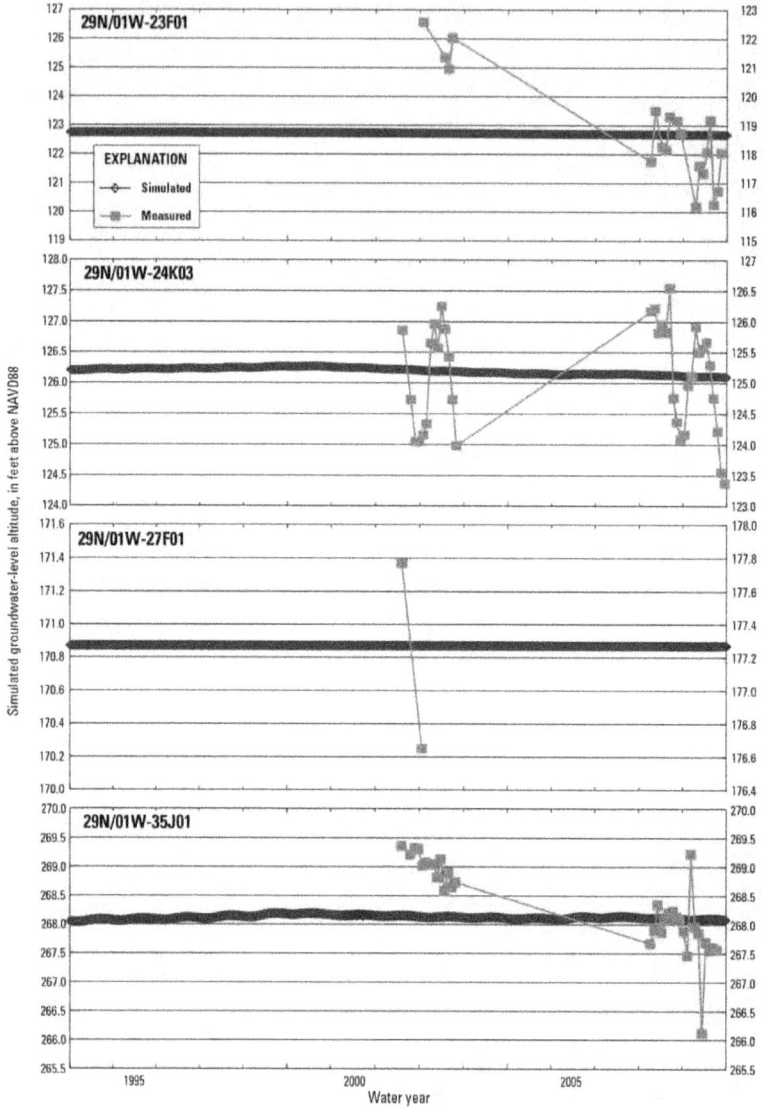

Figure 5*A.*—Continued.

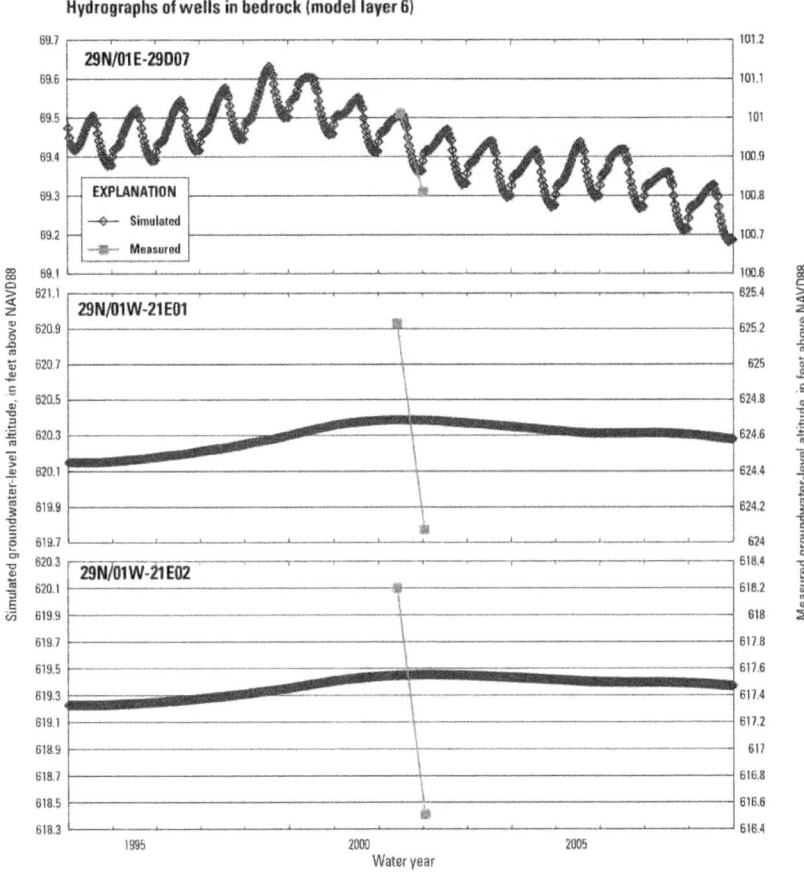

Hydrographs of wells in bedrock (model layer 6)

Figure 5A.—Continued.

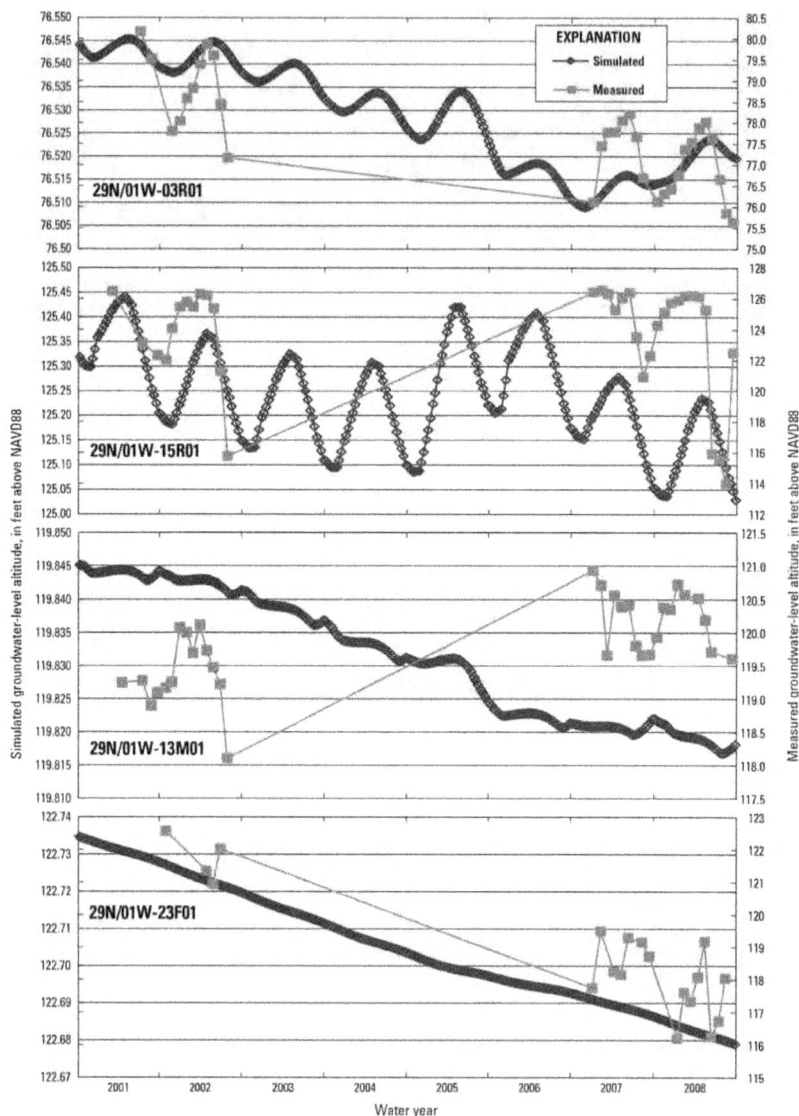

Figure 5*B.*—Continued.

36

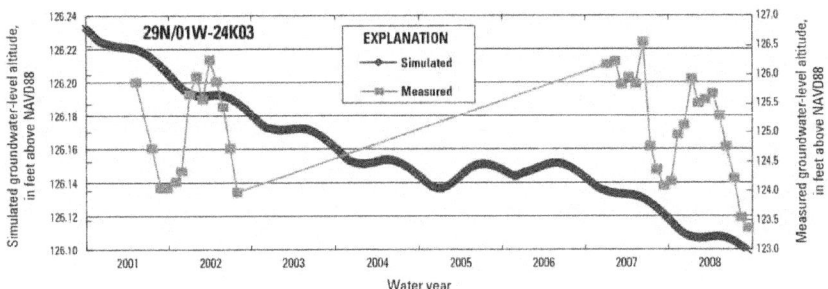

Figure 5B.—Continued.

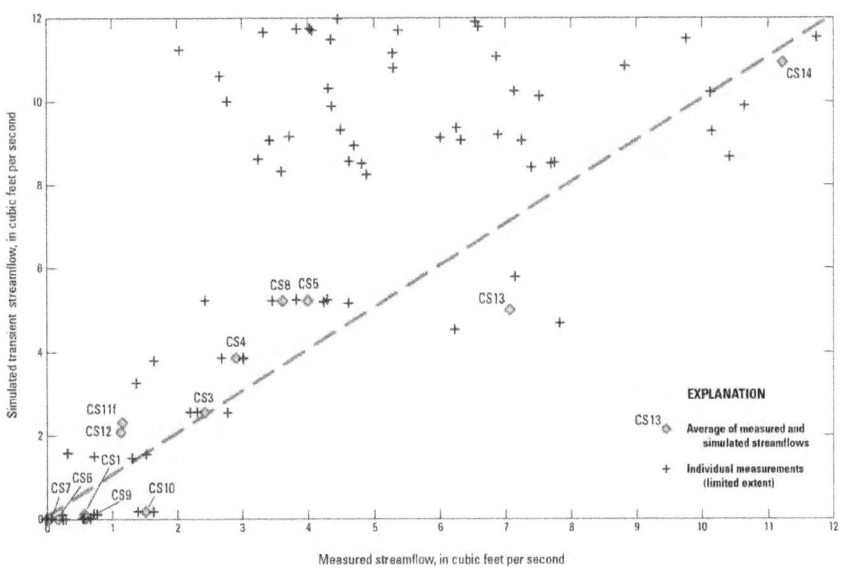

Measured streamflow, in cubic feet per second

Figure 6. Graph showing simulated and measured streamflow from groundwater discharge for the calibrated model for transient conditions, Chimacum Creek Basin and vicinity, Jefferson County, Washington.

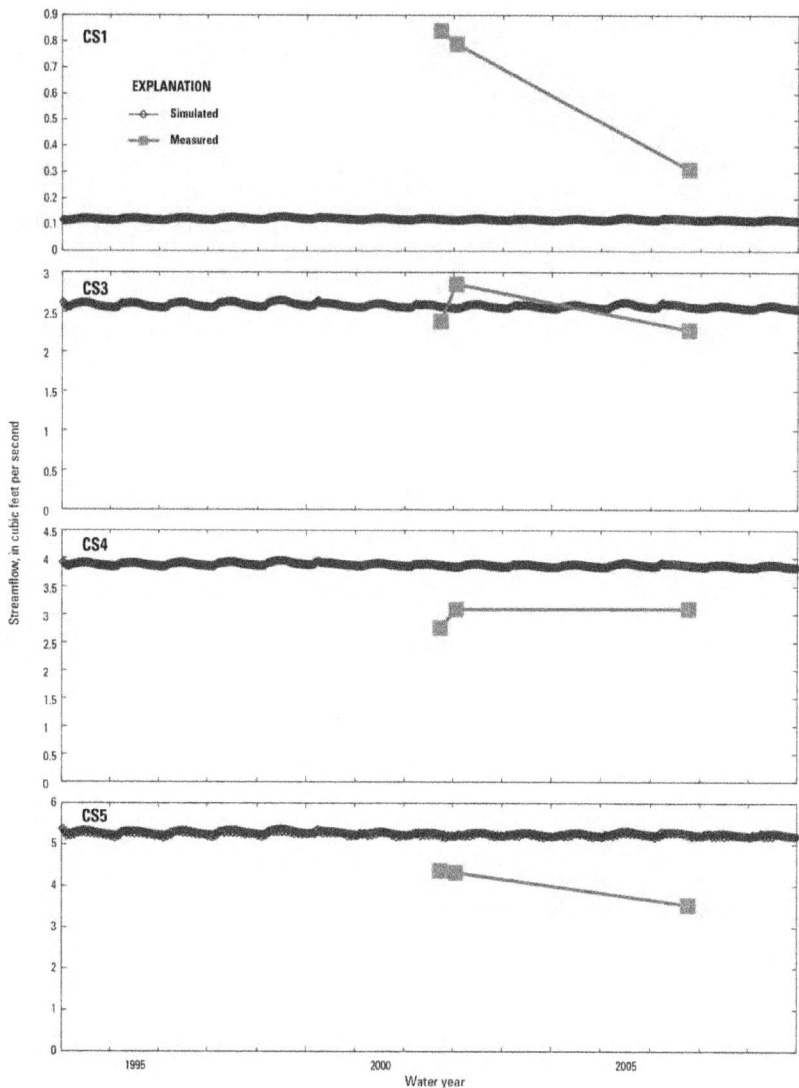

Figure 7. Hydrographs of simulated and measured streamflow from groundwater discharge for the calibrated model for transient conditions, Chimacum Creek Basin and vicinity, Jefferson County, Washington.

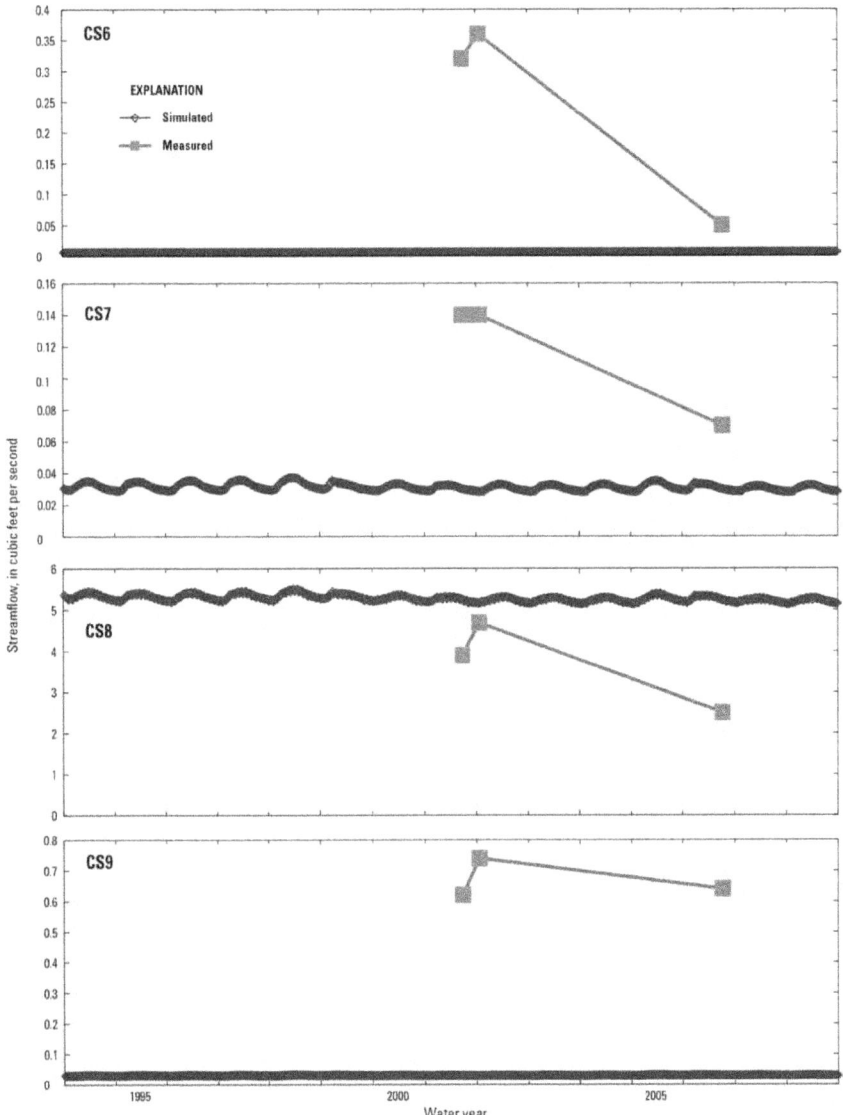

Figure 7.—Continued.

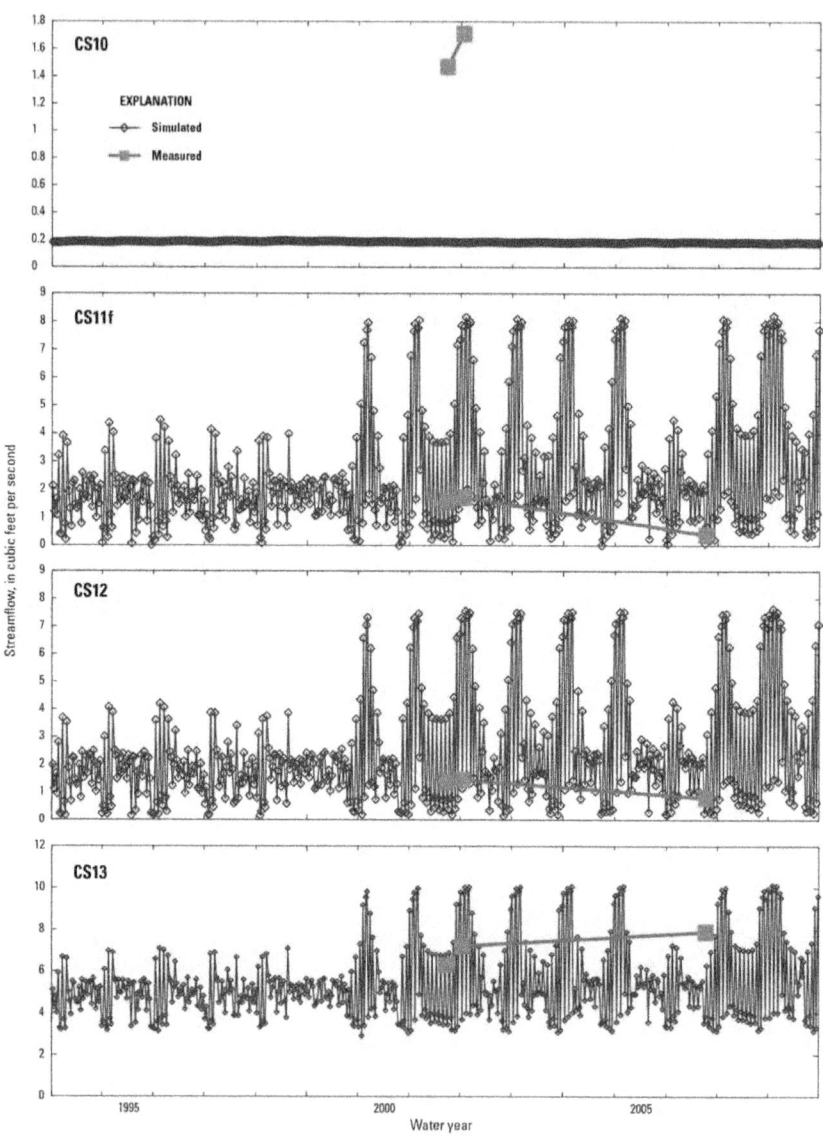

Figure 7.—Continued.

40

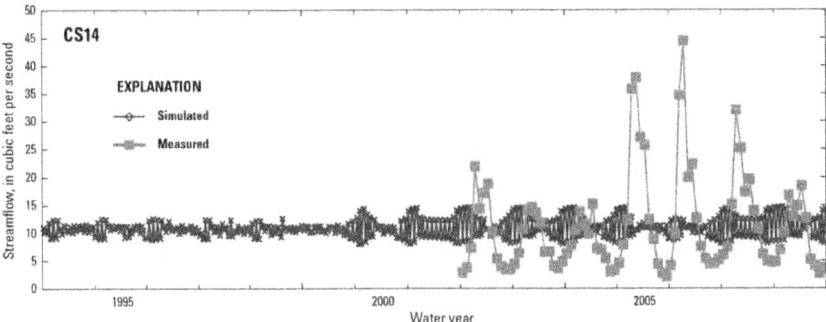

Figure 7.—Continued.

Possible Causes for Poor Calibration

MODFLOW attempts to solve the governing equations of groundwater flow where the unknown variables (groundwater-level altitude, streamflow, hydraulic conductivity, etc.) are more numerous than the known variables. Because of this, MODFLOW, as well as other groundwater- flow models, estimates values for variables, calculates the difference between variables and target values, and adjusts the value of the variable(s) in an iterative process to minimize the difference, or "residual." The model repeats the process, "iterates," until the differences are minimized; it "converges" on the minima. The magnitude of acceptable residuals is set as part of model preparation, and attaining results at or lower than the value set is called convergence. In a steady-state simulation, this process is done once; in a transient simulation, this process is repeated for each of the time intervals ("time steps"), which together cover the entire time period being considered. The transient simulation failed to converge for any time steps, with the largest residuals occurring primarily during the time periods representing late summer, when Chimacum Creek would have lowest flows and would be receiving groundwater discharge in the largest amounts during the course of a year, and for the longest lengths of a stream. The information provided by the model from a failed convergence is limited to the magnitude of changes in heads and residuals for model cells, and the largest of those occurred in cells representing Chimacum Creek. Therefore, it is presumed that the instability and failure to converge is due to aquifer- stream interactions. The MODFLOW STR package was used to simulate cells representing Chimacum Creek, and as part of the solution for each time step, stream stages and cumulative streamflow are estimated. Those estimates of stream stage and cumulative streamflow cascade to downstream cells, further increasing the potential for developing numerical instabilities. Thus, it appeared that oscillation between gaining and losing conditions in Chimacum Creek, and the associated cascade of these changes from upstream to downstream, were the primary cause of the failure to achieve a successful transient calibration. Streamflow loss to groundwater when the water table is below the bottom of the stream channel is a linear function of stream stage. Streamflow loss to groundwater when the water table is above the bottom of the stream but below the stream stage, and streamflow gain from groundwater are functions of both the water-table altitude and the stream stage, both of which the model is attempting to estimate. This was possibly the cause of the numerical instability, which prevented convergence.

Recommendations for Further Study

Although the MODFLOW package STR was considered necessary in order to efficiently simulate and calculate cumulative stream stages and streamflow, which was a calibration target, an alternative package such as RIV could possibly be used with adapted calibration targets that would allow convergence during the calibration process. RIV would not attempt to estimate (and thus, vary) the stream stage, and would not cascade those estimates and changes of those estimates between iterations downstream. The resulting model would perhaps not be as useful as one successfully calibrated using STR, but it may eliminate the instabilities that caused the failure to converge experienced using STR. Additionally, alternate methods of formulating and solving the governing equations in newer versions of MODFLOW, such as MODFLOW-NWT, could be used to attempt to achieve a successful calibration.

Summary

A steady-state groundwater-flow model was developed to evaluate potential future impacts of growth and of water-management strategies on water resources in the Chimacum Creek Basin. The model, the steady-state calibration, and simulation of potential future conditions are reported in Scientific Investigations Report 2013-5160, Numerical Simulation of the Groundwater-Flow System in Chimacum Creek Basin and Vicinity, Jefferson County, Washington. The model covers an area of about 64 square miles on the Olympic Peninsula in northeastern Jefferson County, Washington. The Chimacum Creek Basin drains an area of about 53 square miles and consists of Chimacum Creek and its tributary East Fork Chimacum Creek, which converge near the town of Chimacum and discharge to Port Townsend Bay near the town of Irondale. The geologic setting for Chimacum Creek Basin and the adjacent lands to the west, bordering Discovery Bay, and to the east, bordering Port Townsend Bay and Oak Bay, are typical of the Puget Sound Lowlands; unconsolidated deposits of glacial and interglacial origin are present throughout the study area. Recharge from precipitation is the dominant source of water to the aquifer system. Return flow (recharge resulting from water use) from irrigation and septic systems contribute small amounts of recharge. Discharge primarily is to marine waters below sea level and to Chimacum Creek and its tributaries. Springs, seeps, and wells for public supply, domestic supply, and agriculture comprise the balance of groundwater discharge.

The model is comprised of a grid of 245 columns and 313 rows; cells are a uniform 200 feet per side. There are six model layers, each representing one hydrogeologic unit: (1) Upper Confining unit (UC); (2) Upper Aquifer unit (UA); (3) Middle Confining unit (MC); (4) Lower Aquifer unit (LA); (5) Lower Confining unit (LC); and (6) Bedrock unit (OE). The boundaries of the model coincide with natural topographic, geologic, and hydrologic boundaries except the northern edge. The transient simulation period (October 1994–September 2009) was divided into 180 monthly stress periods to represent temporal variations in recharge, discharge, and storage. Agricultural groundwater withdrawals were apportioned between May and September, as was done for the surface-water diversions. Attempts to calibrate the transient model used head and flow data measured from October 2001 through September 2009 to estimate storage coefficients for (conceptually) unconfined model layers, and stream conductances for 33 stream reaches.

The attempt to calibrate the model to transient conditions was unsuccessful due to instabilities stemming from oscillations in groundwater discharge to recharge from streamflow in Chimacum Creek. The model as calibrated to transient conditions has a mean residual and standard error of 0.06 ±0.45 feet for heads and 0.48 ±0.06 cubic feet per second for flows. Measured fluctuations in groundwater levels were small, typically about 2 feet; similar fluctuations were not observed in the transient simulation, although the expected seasonal fluctuations were observed. The highest simulated streamflows were 33 percent of the measured flows at the most downstream station. Low flows were less well estimated. Because the transient version of the model proved inherently unstable, it was not used to simulate forecast conditions or alternate hydrologic or anthropogenic changes.

Alternate stream simulation packages, such as RIV, could be used to simulate Chimacum Creek in order to achieve an acceptable calibration, although the utility of the resulting model might be less useful than a successful calibration using the package used for this attempt (STR). Additionally, newer versions of MODFLOW, such as MODFLOW-NWT, could prove capable of managing the instabilities resulting from highly varying groundwater/surface-water interactions.

References Cited

Doherty, J., 2003, Ground water model calibration using pilot points and regularization: Ground Water, v. 41, no. 2, p. 170–177.

Doherty, J., 2005, PEST—Model-independent parameter estimation: Corinda, Australia, Watermark Numerical Computing, variously paged.

Doherty, J., and Hunt R.J., 2009, Two statistics for evaluating parameter identifiability and error reduction: Journal of Hydrology, v. 366, no. 1–4, p. 119–127

Harbaugh, A.W., 2005, MODFLOW-2005, the U.S. Geological Survey modular ground-water model—The ground-water flow process: U.S. Geological Survey Techniques and Methods 6-A16, variously paged.

Jones, J.L., Johnson, K.H., and Frans, L.M., 2013, Numerical simulation of the groundwater-flow system in Chimacum Creek Basin and vicinity, Jefferson County, Washington: U.S. Geological Survey Scientific Investigations Report 2013-5160, 79 p. (Also available at http://pubs.usgs.gov/sir/2013/5160.)

Jones, J.L., Welch, W.B., Frans, L.M., and Olsen, T.D., 2011, Hydrogeologic framework, groundwater movement, and water budget in the Chimacum Creek basin and vicinity, Jefferson County, Washington: U.S. Geological Survey Scientific Investigations Report 2011–5129, 28 p. (Also available at *http://pubs.usgs.gov/sir/2011/5129/*.)

National Oceanic and Atmospheric Administration, 2007, Climatological data—Annual summary, Washington: Asheville, North Carolina, National Climatic Data Center, v. 111, no. 13, 30 p.

Parametrix, Inc., Pacific Groundwater Group, Inc., Montgomery Water Group, Inc., and Caldwell and Associates, 2000, Stage 1 technical assessment as of February 2000, Water Resource Inventory Area (WRIA) 17: Jefferson County, Washington, Project No. 553-1820-007, accessed July 28, 2011, at *http://www.ecy.wa.gov/programs/eap/wrias/Planning/docs/063010_wria17_water_supply_de mand.pdf*.

Ritter, D.F., 1978, Process geomorphology: Dubuque, Iowa, William C. Brown Company Publishers, 414 p.